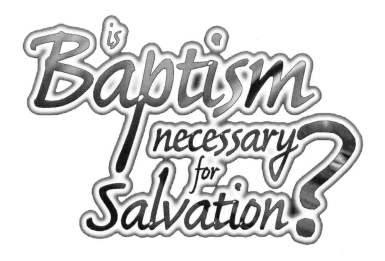

Cougan Collins

Cover design by Jim Nash

Is Baptism Necessary For Salvation?
By Cougan Collins
© 2009 by Cougan Collins

ISBN: 978-0-578-00514-0

Cougan Collins
P.O. Box 65
Lone Grove, OK 73443
http://www.lgchurchofchrist.com

TABLE OF CONTENTS

I dedicate this book to my loving wife, Erica, and my two beautiful daughters. I am also thankful for my mother-in-law, Carol Snyder, Gary Summers, Melba Wallace, and others who helped proof this book.

INTRODUCTION

The Word of God has a lot to say about the topic of baptism. There are six different baptisms mentioned in the New Testament.

First is the baptism of the children of Israel into Moses (1 Cor. 10:1-2; Ex. 14:19ff), which describes how they were surrounded by a wall of water on each side and a cloud. When they came out on the other side of the Red Sea, they were saved from the Egyptians, and they began a new life with Moses as their mediator.

Second is John's baptism, which came from God (Mt. 21:25). Accepting his baptism justified God (Lk. 7:29), but refusing it was to reject the will of God (Lk. 7:30). John's baptism was an immersion in water (Jn. 3:23; Mk. 1:5, 9-10), and He was preparing the way for the Lord. John's baptism had a specific purpose and prerequisites. First, people had to believe in the Messiah that would come after him (Acts 19:4). Second, they had to confess their sins (Mt. 3:6; Mk. 1:5). Third, it was a baptism of repentance (Acts 13:24; 19:4). Fourth, it was a baptism for the forgiveness of sin (Mk. 1:4; Lk. 3:3). John's baptism was also carried out by Jesus' disciples (Jn. 3:22, 26; 4:1-2). However, the authority for his baptism ended when The Great Commission was commanded (Mt. 28:18-19; Acts 19:4-5).

1

Third is the baptism of suffering (Mt. 20:22-23; Mk. 10:38-39), which refers to the overwhelming suffering that Jesus experienced as He was scourged (Mt. 27:26) and crucified (Mt. 27:35). In other words, He was immersed in pain.

Fourth is the baptism of fire (Mt. 3:11; Lk. 3:16). Some think the baptism of the Holy Spirit and fire are the same thing, but they are not. John was talking to sincere and insincere people. When he said Jesus would baptize them with fire, he was talking about the eternal punishment that all the wicked will be immersed in. This is the reason John said: "His winnowing fan *is* in His hand, and He will thoroughly clean out His threshing floor, and gather His wheat into the barn; but He will burn up the chaff with unquenchable fire" (Mt. 3:12). Those who claim the apostles were baptized with fire on the day of Pentecost have misunderstood Acts 2:4 because it describes divided tongues that looked like fire and sat upon each apostle. So, this does not describe being baptized by fire at all.

Fifth is the baptism of the Holy Spirit, which was spoken of by John the Baptist (Mt. 3:11; Lk. 3:16). As we examine more Scriptures, we will discover that Holy Spirit baptism was a promise to the apostles, and Jesus would administer it (Lk. 24:49; Jn. 16:5-15; Acts 1:8). Jesus clarified that John's teaching about the baptism of the Holy Spirit applied to the apostles when He said to His apostles: "For John truly baptized with water, but you shall be baptized with the Holy Spirit not many days from now" (Acts 1:5). This promise was fulfilled in Acts 2:1-4, which proved that Jesus was sitting at the right hand of God (Acts 2:33). The only other recorded instance of Holy Spirit baptism happened at Cornelius's household (Acts 11:15). Since Jesus was the only one who could administer this baptism, which was a promise and not a command, it cannot be the baptism that Jesus commanded in The Great Commission.

2

Sixth is the baptism of The Great Commission (Mt. 28:19; Mk. 16:16), which is administered by humans. Paul said there was one baptism when he wrote to the Ephesians (Eph. 4:5). That one baptism is the baptism of The Great Commission. It was taught at the birth of the church as being for the forgiveness of sin (Acts 2:38). It is an immersion in water (Acts 8:38; 10:47), and it saves a person (1 Pet. 3:21). Before a person is baptized, he must believe that Jesus is the Son of God (Jn. 3:16), repent (Lk. 13:3), and confess Jesus as Lord (Rom. 10:9-10). Even though this baptism is administered by others, what takes place at a person's baptism is a work of God (Col. 2:12). When a person is baptized, he is buried with Jesus, united with Him, raised alive with Him, and his sins are forgiven by the blood of Jesus (Rom. 6:1-11; Col. 2:12-13; Acts 12:38; 22:16; Rev. 1:5). At the point of baptism, we are added to the church by God (1 Cor. 12:13; Acts 2:47).

Six different baptisms are mentioned in the New Testament, but our main focus will be the baptism of The Great Commission because it is the one that saves. Many in the religious world teach that baptism is not necessary for salvation. Instead, they would say that baptism is something a person does after he is saved. This book will challenge that view and prove that baptism is necessary for salvation.

While this book will focus on baptism, please understand that baptism is not more important than faith, repentance, or confessing Jesus as Lord, but it is equally important. All these things work together to bring about salvation, and one will not work without the other.

To get the most out of this book, one needs to open his Bible and read all the Scripture references in context. I do not want anyone to take me at my word just because I have written a book. Instead, my desire is that everyone will be like the Bereans and search the Scriptures daily to see if these things are so (Acts 17:11). It would also help if everyone will study this topic with an open mind and be willing to change if their view is wrong.

Baptism is a serious topic that deserves your attention. If baptism is the point at which a person is saved and you were taught that a person is baptized after they are saved, then you were never baptized for the remission of sin, which means you are lost. I believe this is the greatest trick the devil has pulled off because a person can live like a Christian and act like a Christian but still belong to the devil because he has never had his sins removed in the watery grave of baptism (Mt. 7:21ff). Since baptism makes the difference between being saved and being lost, everyone should read and study this topic closely.

All Scripture *is* given by inspiration of God, and *is* profitable for doctrine, for reproof, for correction, for instruction in righteousness, that the man of God may be complete, thoroughly equipped for every good work (2 Tim. 3:16-17).

4

YOU MUST BE BORN AGAIN
John 3:3-5

1

Nicodemus was curious about Jesus because He had performed many signs (Jn. 3:2). So, he came to Jesus at night to find out more about Him. Notice what Jesus told Him in the following verses:

Jesus answered and said to him, "Most assuredly, I say to you, unless one is born again, he cannot see the kingdom of God." Nicodemus said to Him, "How can a man be born when he is old? Can he enter a second time into his mother's womb and be born?" Jesus answered, "Most assuredly, I say to you, unless one is born of water and the Spirit, he cannot enter the kingdom of God (Jn. 3:3-5).

Jesus' answer confused Nicodemus because all he could think about was the physical. He knew that he belonged to the physical kingdom of Israel because all Jews were considered to be part of God's chosen nation. Now Jesus is telling him that a person must be born again or he cannot enter the kingdom of God or even see it.

In verse 4, Nicodemus is trying to make sense of Jesus' statement from a physical point of view, which is the reason he asked: "How can a man be born when he is old? Can he

5

enter a second time into his mother's womb and be born?" He thought Jesus' statement was crazy because he knew it was impossible to be physically reborn. So, Jesus restates what He said to help Nicodemus understand that He was talking about a spiritual rebirth and not a physical one. Jesus clearly states that a person cannot enter the kingdom of God, which John the Baptist said was at hand (Mk. 1:15), unless he is born again. To be born again, a person must be born of water and the spirit. Since, these two elements are necessary for salvation, it is important we take a closer look at what they are and how we are born again.

First, let's take a look at the word *water* and how it relates to being born again. The word *water* comes from the Greek word *hudor*, which simply means "water." So, water is one of the elements necessary to be born again, which refers to baptism. In fact, we can see that water is required for baptism. For instance, when John was baptizing, he baptized with water (Mk. 1:8-10; Jn. 3:23). When the apostles and disciples were carrying out The Great Commission, they baptized with water (Acts 8:36-39; 10:47). When Paul wrote to the Ephesians, he declared there was only one baptism that saves (Eph. 4:4-5), and Peter taught that one baptism is by water (1 Pet. 3:20-21). In Romans 6, Paul described baptism as a burial where we die to our sins, and we are made alive with Jesus (Col. 2:13), which is exactly what Jesus described to Nicodemus about being born again. At the point of baptism, our old man of sin is put to death as we are buried under the water. When we are raised from the water, we are *born again* as a new creature of Christ without our sins.

The evidence I have provided proves that water baptism is one of the essential elements necessary to enter the kingdom of God to be saved. In fact, all the early writers, known as the *church fathers*, agree that John 3:5 is talking about water baptism.

In his monumental work, *History of Infant Baptism*, William Wall, a leading scholar in the Church of England, asserted that not a single writer of antiquity denied the identification of the "water" of John 3:5 with baptism. He suggested that John Calvin was the first to disassociate the two items, and that Calvin even conceded that his interpretation was "new" (Oxford, 1862, Vol. I, p. 443) (Jackson, christiancourier.com).

Not only does the Bible prove that Jesus is talking about water baptism, all these early non-inspired writers understood that Jesus was talking about water baptism as well.

Second, let's examine the word *spirit* and how it relates to being born again. We need to keep in mind there is only one birth, and it consists of water and spirit. Therefore, there are not two births as some teach. Jesus is teaching that the Holy Spirit is involved in being born again, but the question is, how? To answer this question, we must go beyond this one passage and look at the whole counsel of God. When we do this, we will learn that the Holy Spirit instructs us through the Word of God on how to be saved, which is the role that He plays in our being born again.

The Holy Spirit's primary purpose was to reveal the Word of God to us (Jn. 14:26; 16:13-15). He spoke through some of Jesus' disciples, who in turn recorded these revelations to us in our Bibles (2 Tim. 3:16-17; 1 Cor. 2:12-13; 2 Pet. 1:20-21). So there was no confusion, these disciples would prove they were speaking the Word of God by the inspiration of the Holy Spirit by backing it up with a miracle (Mk. 16:20; Acts 2:43; 5:12; 6:8; 8:13; Rom. 15:19). Jesus said: "It is the Spirit who gives life; the flesh profits nothing. The words that I speak to you are spirit, and *they* are life" (Jn. 6:63). Paul referred to the New Testament as being of the Spirit (2 Cor.

3:6). The Holy Spirit works through the Word to teach us how to enter the kingdom of God (Eph. 6:17). It is through the Word, or we could say by the Spirit, that we learn how to be saved (1 Pet. 1:23; Rom. 1:16, Jam. 1:18, 21).

To further show how the Holy Spirit works in our conversion with water baptism, take a look at the following parallel passages:

Husbands, love your wives, just as Christ also loved the church and gave Himself for her, that He might <u>sanctify and cleanse</u> her with the <u>washing of water</u> <u>by the word</u> (Ephesians 5:25-26)

Notice the three elements: the word, washing of water, and cleanse. *The word* is a reference to the Word of God. *Washing of water* refers to water baptism. *Sanctify and cleanse* refers to being saved with our sins being removed.

...He <u>saved us</u>, through the <u>washing of regeneration</u> and <u>renewing of the Holy Spirit</u> (Titus 3:5).

Notice the three elements: Holy Spirit, washing of regeneration, and saved. *Renewing of the Holy Spirit* refers to how the Holy Spirit works through the Word to save us (James 1:21). Washing is defined as "Washing, cleansing; water" (UBS Lexicon). *Regeneration* is defined as "a new birth or renewal or restoration of life after death" (Thayer). So, *washing of regeneration* is referring to water baptism, and *saved* means salvation.

For by <u>one Spirit</u> we were all <u>baptized</u> into <u>one body</u> (1 Cor. 12:13).

Notice the three elements: Spirit, baptized, one body. Notice that Paul said, "By one Spirit" and not "With one Spirit." This is important because it proves the baptism being spoken of is not Holy Spirit baptism because it is by the Holy Spirit.

8

The Holy Spirit instructs us through the Word that we must be baptized in water into the name of Jesus for the remission of our sins (Acts 2:38). So, *baptism* refers to water baptism. *One body* is the same as saying the kingdom because the body is the church (Col. 1:18, 24), and the church is the same as the kingdom (Mt. 16:18-19). Now, examine the chart below:

John 3:5	Spirit	Water	Kingdom
Eph. 5:26	Word	Water	Cleansed
Tit. 3:5	Holy Spirit	Washing	Saved
1 Cor. 12:13	Spirit	Baptized	Body

All these verses prove that the Holy Spirit works through the Word of God to teach us what we must do to be born again, which includes: believing Jesus is the Son of God (Jn. 8:24), repenting (Lk. 13:3), confessing Jesus as Lord (Rom. 10:9-10), and being baptized (Acts 2:38; 1 Pet. 3:21; Acts 22:16). When we obey the Holy Spirit's instructions, we are added to the kingdom by God (Acts 2:47), which is Jesus' church or body (Col. 1:18, 24) that He will save (Eph. 5:23).

Whenever we are born again, we receive the gift of the Holy Spirit (Acts 2:38; 5:32), which means we have been sealed by Him (Eph. 1:13; 4:30; 2 Cor. 1:22). The word *seal* means: "To mark with a seal as a means of identification, *mark, seal* so that the mark denoting ownership also carries with it the protection of the owner" (BDAG). This definition fits perfectly with The Great Commission (Mt. 28:19), which teaches that we are baptized into the name of, or into the possession of the Father, the Son, and the Holy Spirit. This seal is our guarantee of a home in heaven if we remain faithful (Rev. 2:10). Just as the Holy Spirit was a witness for Jesus (1 Jn. 5:6), He bears witness that we are children of God (Rom. 8:16). Once we are born again, we are considered to be the temple of God, and all three members of the Godhead will dwell in us (Holy Spirit: 1 Cor. 3:16; 6:19; Rom. 8:9, 11; Father: 2 Cor. 6:16; Jn. 14:23; Jesus: Rom. 8:10; 2 Cor. 13:5; Jn. 6:56). How do they dwell in us? It is by our faith (Eph. 3:17). We can know they dwell in us just like we can know our sins are being removed and we are being united with Christ at the point of baptism (Col. 2:12). It is by our faith in the working of God.

Jesus taught Nicodemus and us a valuable lesson. If we want to be saved and able to enter the kingdom of God, we must be born again by obeying the instructions of the Holy Spirit, which includes being water baptized in the name of Jesus for the remission of our sins.

Now I want to deal with the objections that some have with these verses.

1. Some teach that Jesus is talking about Holy Spirit baptism. I have already proven the baptism that saves is water baptism, but let's take a look as some more reasons this cannot be talking about Holy Spirit baptism. Holy Spirit baptism only occurs two times in Scripture, and it was followed with the miraculous ability to speak in another language. First, at the day of Pentecost (Acts 2) and second, at Cornelius's house (Acts 10). Holy Spirit baptism was a promise that Jesus would administer, and He only promised it to His apostles (Lk. 24:49; Acts 1:4; 2:33). If Jesus was talking about Holy Spirit baptism, then it would be necessary for every single person to receive it to enter the kingdom of God. Again, we only have two cases of it in Scripture.

If Holy Spirit baptism is essential for salvation and water baptism is not, then we will have a difficult time explaining why Philip only baptized the people of Samaria in water, and then left them in an unsaved condition (Acts 8:14-16). The only other way a person could receive the miraculous gifts of the Holy Spirit was by the laying on of hands by an apostle, which is the why Peter and John had to go to Samaria. This ability died out with the last apostle, and it is not available today. If Holy Spirit baptism was necessary, then why did Ananias tell Paul to get up and get himself baptized (Acts 22:16)? If Holy Spirit baptism is what saves, the Holy Spirit could have baptized Paul right then and there even if he was standing on his head. It should be obvious that water baptism is what Jesus is talking about in this verse because it was commanded, which means we are to obey it and administer it (Mt. 28:18). Water baptism was done throughout the book of Acts because it is the one baptism that saves (Eph. 4:4-5).

2. Some teach the word *water* is talking about the amniotic fluid that surrounds a baby in the womb, and the spirit is referring to being born of the Spirit, which brings us back to Holy Spirit baptism. First, it would not make sense for Jesus to say that you must be born from the water of your mother because who isn't born from their mother? If Jesus wanted us to know that Holy Spirit baptism was necessary, He would have said you must be born of the Spirit. Second, Jesus had the chance to explain to Nicodemus that He had already accomplished the first element in verse 5. Instead, He said he must be born of water and Spirit. Obviously, Jesus was letting him know that he had not experienced this new birth of water and Spirit. Third, the word *water* in this text is never used in the Bible to refer to childbirth, which proves the word *water* in this verse does not refer to childbirth.

3. Some have even taught the word *water* represents the semen of a man, which is ridiculous. However, everything stated in point two proves the word *water* in our text cannot be referring to such a thing.

4. Finally, some teach the word *water* refers to the Word of God. However, several passages have already been citied that prove the Holy Spirit works through the Word of God (Jn. 6:63; Eph. 6:17; 2 Tim. 3:16-17; 1 Cor. 2:12-13; 2 Cor. 3:6; 2 Pet. 1:20-21). Besides, there is nothing in verses 3-5 that

would cause us to view the water as symbolic of something else.

In conclusion, we have examined the first reference to water baptism that Jesus would command under the new covenant, which is necessary to enter the kingdom of God. The only way we can be born again and set free from our sins is by obeying the instructions of the Holy Spirit, which includes believing Jesus is the Son of God, repenting, confessing Jesus as Lord, and being water baptized in the name of Jesus for the remission of sins. Jesus' instructions to Nicodemus prove that water baptism is necessary for salvation.

Questions

1. What two elements are necessary to be born again?
2. How do we know Jesus was talking about water baptism in John 3:5?
3. How is the Holy Spirit involved in being born again?
4. Can we enter the kingdom of God without being born again?
5. What other views do people have about being born again?

12

THE GREAT COMMISSION
MATTHEW 28:18-20

2

After Jesus' glorious resurrection from the dead, He appeared to His disciples to show them He had risen from the dead. While some of them had trouble believing their own eyes, Jesus was alive and He had a message for them that would change their lives forever.

And Jesus came and spoke to them, saying, "All authority has been given to Me in heaven and on earth. "Go therefore and make disciples of all the nations, baptizing them in the name of the Father and of the Son and of the Holy Spirit, "teaching them to observe all things that I have commanded you; and lo, I am with you always, even to the end of the age." Amen (Mt. 28:18-20).

His disciples may have thought their work was finished when Christ was crucified on the cruel cross, but they found out their work has just begun. Jesus had prepared His disciples earlier for this momentous occasion as He sent them out on a limited commission to the Jews only (Mt. 10:5ff). Now the command was to go out to all nations, which would include both Jews and Gentiles.

Let's take a closer look at Jesus' words. First, He said: "All authority has been given to me in heaven and earth." In this statement, Jesus is showing His Divine nature and that He is the Son of God. The word *authority* comes from the Greek word *exousia*, which means: "The power of him whose will and commands must be submitted to by others and obeyed" (Thayer). Only Jesus could make such a statement because He gave up the riches of His heavenly home to become human (2 Cor. 8:9; Phil. 2:5ff; John 1:1ff) and to be tempted, yet He did not sin (Heb. 4:15). He remained faithful to God the Father all the days of His life, including the intense suffering and shame He endured surrounding His crucifixion (Phil. 2:8ff). As proof of His faithfulness, God raised Him from the dead, which is reason He could say He has all authority over heaven and earth. So, every person is subject to Jesus' authority except for the Father (1 Cor. 15:27). When Jesus ascended to the Father, He sat down at His right side, and He poured out the Holy Spirit onto His apostles, which proved His reign as King had begun (Acts 2:1-36). The church/kingdom began on the day of Pentecost, and Jesus is its head on the earth and in heaven (Eph. 1:22-23). This is the reason we should not have earthly headquarters, as some in the religious world have, because Christ is our head and authority. Also, some claim that Jesus' kingdom is still yet to come. However, that is not logical because Jesus has all authority over heaven and earth, and He is called "King of kings and Lord of lords" (1 Tim. 6:15). If His kingdom is still in the future, then what does He have authority over? What is He King of? The Scriptures clearly state that He is reigning over His kingdom right now with all authority, and He will hand over His kingdom to the Father when He comes again (1 Cor. 15:24ff).

After Jesus proclaimed His authority, He commanded His disciples: "Go therefore and make disciples of all the nations." While Jesus directed this command to His disciples of that day, this same command is to be followed by all Christians. All Christians should be doing what they can to reach the lost and lead people to Christ. Notice, the command is to "make disciples." The word *disciple* comes from the Greek word *matheteuo*, which means: "To be the disciple of one; to follow his precepts and instruction; to teach" (Thayer). Simply put, a disciple is one who is taught and follows the teaching of another. So, one must be taught before he can become a disciple of Christ, which is exactly what Jeremiah prophesied.

"Behold, the days are coming, says the LORD, when I will make a new covenant with the house of Israel and with the house of Judah -- "not according to the covenant that I made with their fathers in the day that I took them by the hand to lead them out of the land of Egypt, My covenant which they broke, though I was a husband to them, says the LORD. "But this is the covenant that I will make with the house of Israel after those days, says the LORD: I will put My law in their minds, and write it on their hearts; and I will be their God, and they shall be My people. "No more shall every man teach his neighbor, and every man his brother, saying, 'Know the LORD,' for they all shall know Me, from the least of them to the greatest of them, says the LORD. For I will forgive their iniquity, and their sin I will remember no more" (Jer. 31:31-34).

Under the Law of Moses a Jew was born a child of God, and a male child was circumcised on the 8th day (Gen. 17:12-13). As he grew up, he was taught about God and how he needs to obey His commands. However, Jeremiah is teaching that this process would change under the new covenant that we are under now. Under the new covenant, no one is born a child of God. Instead, he must learn about God first and then choose to accept God's grace by obeying His commands. Therefore, a person must be taught before he can become a disciple of Christ.

To prove this principle further, consider the following points:

- A person must have faith to be pleasing to God (Heb. 11:6).
- A person can only have faith in God if he hears the Word of God (Rom. 10:17).
- Jesus said: "And you shall *know the truth*, and the truth shall make you free" (Jn. 8:32, emph. mine).
- Jesus said: "No one can come to Me unless the Father who sent Me draws him; and I will raise him up at the last day. "It is written in the prophets, 'And *they shall all be taught* by God.' Therefore everyone who has *heard and learned* from the Father comes to Me" (Jn. 6:44-45, emph. mine).

Many other passages could be given, but these are enough to prove that a person must be taught before he can become a disciple of Christ. This truth proves that infant baptism is invalid and unscriptural. Neither an infant nor a young child has the cognitive ability to be taught in such a way for them to understand what it means to be a disciple of Christ.

Jesus told His disciples to make disciples of "all nations." This would include all nationalities because God does not show partiality (Acts 10:34-35; Gal. 3:28ff). He wants all humans to come to a knowledge of the truth and be saved (1 Tim. 2:4; 2 Pet. 3:9). These verses can also be used to show Calvinism's doctrine on selective grace is not true because salvation is available for everyone. At first, Jesus' disciples did not fully understand that all nations included the Gentiles until several years later. God revealed this truth to Peter and his companions at the conversion of Cornelius's household (Acts 10). From that point forward, the Word of God was eventually preached to everyone (Col. 1:6, 23).

As we get back to Jesus' commands, we learn that teaching is not the only thing necessary for becoming a disciple. He also made baptism necessary as well. He commanded them: *"Baptizing* them in the name of the Father and of the Son and of the Holy Spirit, *teaching* them to observe all things that I have commanded you" (emph. mine). Jesus is teaching us that teaching and baptism are necessary to become a disciple of Christ, which can be proven by examining the grammar of the original Greek. Both Greek words for *baptizing* and *teaching* are present participles, which shows their action takes place at the same time as the main verb "make disciples." So, both teaching and baptizing are necessary to complete the action of the main verb, "make disciples." *The Pulpit Commentary* explains it this way: "The present participle denotes the mode of initiation into discipleship. Make them disciples by baptizing them" (The Pulpit Commentary on Mt. 28:19). The English and Greek grammar proves that Jesus commanded His disciples to teach and baptize to make a disciple.

Jesus command to teach and baptize is to be carried out by humans because we can teach, and we can baptize someone. The baptism commanded by Jesus was to continue until the end of the age. The only baptism this could refer to is water baptism and not Holy Spirit baptism as some claim. Holy Spirit baptism was a promise (Acts 2:33) that Jesus would administer (Mt. 3:11), and we only have two recorded instances of this happening in the Bible. The first instance was on the day of Pentecost (Acts 2), and the second one was at the house of Cornelius (Acts 10 - 11). Since Holy Spirit baptism was a promise administered by Jesus, it cannot be the baptism commanded in The Great Commission because a person cannot obey a promise. However, we can baptize someone in water, and that is what we see happening throughout the book of Acts. There should be no doubt that water baptism is under consideration here.

Several more interesting points can be observed from Jesus' command to baptize "into the name of the name of the Father and of the Son and of the Holy Spirit." First, we need to examine the phrase, *into the name of* and what it means.

Wayne Jackson notes:

> The expression "into the name" (*eis to onoma*) is interesting. In New Testament Greek it signified that "the one who is baptized becomes the possession of and comes under the protection of" the one into whose name he is immersed (Arndt & Gingrich, p. 575) ("The Great Commission According to Matthew" www.christiancourier.com).

Also consider this quote:

> In the Greek papyri, which is that from which we get the New Testament, "into the name of" was a common phrase for the transference of ownership." That is documented by Stephen L. Keiger in his "ARCHAEOLOGY IN THE NEW TESTAMENT (Wharton 37).

These definitions teach us how important baptism is because when a person is baptized into the name of the Father, the Son, and the Holy Ghost, he becomes God's possession, and he is under His protection. Without baptism, this transfer of ownership and union with God cannot occur, which means a person cannot be a disciple of Christ without baptism.

Paul brings some clarity to this in 1 Corinthians 1 where he taught against dividing the Lord's church. After He taught there is only one church, he made the following statement about baptism:

For it has been declared to me concerning you, my brethren, by those of Chloe's household, that there are contentions among you. Now I say this, that each of you says, "I am of Paul," or "I am of Apollos," or "I am of Cephas," or "I am of Christ." Is Christ divided? Was Paul crucified for you? Or were you baptized in the name of Paul? (1 Cor. 1:11).

Paul is stressing that Christ was crucified for us, and we should not divide the one church He established. Also, we should not exalt a human above Christ by calling ourselves after that person because the church belongs to the Lord (Mt. 16:18); He purchased it with his own blood (Acts 20:7). Finally, Paul teaches that baptism is what makes it possible for us to say, "I am of Christ," which means that we belong to Him.

The second interesting thing about Jesus' command to baptize "into the name of the Father and of the Son and of the Holy Spirit" is that it shows the Trinity of the Godhead, which is even more obvious when we look at the original Greek language. The general rule in Greek grammar is that, when a definite article is present before a word, it identifies it as an individual or a specific thing. However, when the article is absent before a word, it shows its nature or quality.

In Wayne Jackson's book, *Treasures from the Greek New Testament for the English Reader*, he gives several examples of this general rule. However, we will just observe one of them. He wrote:

> In John 4, at Jacob's well, Jesus had an extended conversation with a Samaritan woman. Frequently throughout the narrative she is referred to as "the woman," because a definite female is in view (4:9, 11, 15, etc.). When the disciples came upon this scene, after returning

from a nearby city for food ... (4:27) ... The disciples were surprised that he "was talking with a woman" – woman in terms of gender; any woman (68).

First, *the woman* in verse 9 shows that this specific woman was being referred to as an individual. However, the second use of the word *woman* in verse 27 without the definite article *the*, simply refers to any woman. In Matthew 28:19, all three persons that make up the Godhead have the definite article *the* in front of them which proves that each of them is an individual that makes up the triune nature of God. Now if the passage had only said the Father, Son and Holy Spirit without the definite article before each name, then all three of these could have been referring to one person. Since that is not the case, this is a great passage that refutes the doctrine that states that the Father, the Son, and the Holy Spirit are all the same person.

Next Jesus commands: "Teaching them to observe all things that I have commanded you." As already noted, teaching must occur before we can become a disciple of Christ, and there are certain things we must know and understand to become a disciple of Christ. For instance, we must understand that we are sinners who are separated from God (Rom. 3:23; Isa. 59:1-2). We must believe in Jesus' death, burial, and resurrection, and that He is the only way to heaven (Jn. 14:6). Once we believe that Jesus is the Son of God, and we realize that we are lost without Him; we must be taught to repent (Luke 13:3), and we must turn away from our old lifestyle by living our life according to God's Word. Also, we must confess Jesus as our Lord and continue to confess Him as Lord (Rom. 10:10). Finally, we must be baptized in the name of Jesus (by His authority) for the remission of our sins (Acts 2:38). At the point of baptism we enter into the possession of God, and we are added to the one church by Him (Acts 2:47). When we understand this basic principle of Christianity, we have the knowledge and ability to become a disciple of Christ. Once we choose to accept God's plan of salvation by submitting to God's authority, we must continue to be taught and learn as much as we can about God's commands (2 Tim. 2:15; 2 Pet. 3:18). However, there is more to salvation than just knowing the commands of God because we must live by them faithfully until the day we die (Rev. 2:10).

Finally, Jesus said: "And lo, I am with you always, even to the end of the age." While Jesus was speaking to His apostles, His message applies to us today, and it teaches us that Jesus is with us and He is watching over us until the end of the age when He comes again. These promises are made to Christians in several other passages as well (Rom. 8:28; Heb. 13:5-6; 1 Pet. 3:12). What a comforting thought to know that our God will always be there for us.

The following charts will help us to see the whole counsel of God at work. This first chart will show everything the Gospel accounts say about The Great Commission.

THE GREAT COMMISSION

Mt. 28:18-20	Teach			Baptize	Make Disciples
Mark 16:15-16	Preach	Be-lieve		Baptized	Saved
Luke 24:46-47	Preach		Repen-tance	Remission of Sins	Saved
John 20:21-23	Preach				Saved
All together	Preach	Be-lieve	Repent	Be Bap-tized for The Re-mission of Sins	Makes a Saved Disciple

This chart shows everything Jesus commanded about The Great Commission. The only thing left out is confessing Jesus

21

as Lord. However, we can know that confession is part of The Great Commission, which leads people to salvation, because it is necessary to be saved (Mt. 10:32-33; Rom. 10:9-10). As we put all this together, we learn that we must preach/teach people that they must believe, repent, confess, and be baptized for the remission of their sins. When a person chooses not to accept all that Jesus has commanded on how to be saved, then that person is defying Jesus who has all authority over heaven and earth.

To further illustrate how Jesus' disciples followed His commands of The Great Commission, please note the following chart of conversions in the book of Acts on the next page.

CONVERSIONS IN ACTS

Preaching	Believed	Repented	Confessed	Baptized/Saved
Pentecost (Acts 2:14ff)	Implied (vs. 37, 41)	Repent (vs. 37-38)		Taught (v. 38) Baptized (v. 41)
Samaria (Acts 8:5ff)	Believed (vs. 12, 13)			Baptized (vs. 12-13, 16)
The Eunuch (Acts 8:35-39)	Taught and Believed (v. 37)		Confessed (v. 37)	Baptized (v. 38)
Saul (Acts 9, 22, 26)	Implied (Acts 9:6, 22:10)	Implied (Acts 9:9, 11)	Implied (Acts 9:6, 22:10)	Taught (Acts 22:16) Baptized (Acts 9:18)
Cornelius (Acts 10-11)	Taught (Acts 10:43)	Implied (Acts 11:18)		Commanded (Acts 10:47-48)
Lydia (Acts 16:13)	Implied (v. 14)			Baptized (v. 15)
The Jailer (Acts 16:31ff)	Taught (v. 31)			Baptized (v. 33)
Corinthians (Acts 18:8)	Believed (v. 8)			Baptized (v. 8)
Ephesians (Acts 19:1ff)	Taught (v. 4)			Baptized (vs. 5)

This chart shows how Jesus' disciples obeyed The Great Commission. In every one of these conversions, preach-

23

ing/teaching and baptism occurred. Even though belief, repentance, and confession are not specifically named in each instance, they are implied. When we combine the commands Jesus gave at The Great Commission and compare them to the conversions in the book of Acts, we should not have any problem understanding what it takes to become a disciple of Christ. We must hear the Word of God (Rom. 10:17), believe that Jesus is the Son of God (Jn. 8:24), repent (Luke 13:3), confess Jesus as Lord (Rom. 10:9-10), and be baptized in the name of Jesus for the remission of our sins (Acts 2:38). Dear reader, it is up to you to either receive these words with gladness, and become saved, or refuse them and remain in your sins, separated from God. Choose this day whom will you serve (Josh. 24:15).

Questions

1. Discuss what it means for Jesus to have all authority in heaven and earth.
2. Does the command "Go therefore and make disciples of all nations" apply to us today?
3. Explain how a Jew became a child of God under the Old Testament and how a person becomes a child of God under the New Testament.
4. What two things are necessary to make a disciple?
5. How can we know that Jesus was not commanding Holy Spirit baptism?
6. What is the significance of being baptized in the name of the Father, the Son, and the Holy Spirit?
7. How do the conversions in Acts prove the necessity of baptism?

And He said to them, "Go into all the world and preach the gospel to every creature. "He who believes and is baptized will be saved; but he who does not believe will be condemned (Mk. 16:15-16).

We examined The Great Commission in the previous chapter, but I want to take a closer look at Mark's account, specifically verse 16. This verse proves that baptism is essential for salvation and everyone with an honest heart can see that it does. Before we look at the verse itself, I want to give several examples that will help us see how easy this verse is to understand.

Suppose a radio announcer said: "If you will drive down to the Toyota dealership and be baptized, you will receive a new car. If you do not drive down, you will miss out on a new car." What does a person have to do to receive a new car? He has to drive to the dealership and be baptized. Both of these are necessary. If this was a real announcement, hundreds of people would take advantage of this offer, and they would not have any problem understanding what they must do to receive a new car.

Suppose I said: "If you will stand up and shake my hand, I will give you a thousand dollars." What would a person have to do to receive the money? He would have to stand up and shake my hand. If he stood up and did not shake my hand, would I have to give him the money? No, because he did not shake my hand.

These are simply examples everyone can understand, and it should be just as easy for everyone to understand what Jesus said: "He who believes and is baptized will be saved; but he who does not believe will be condemned." When I was growing up, I enjoyed watching cartoons. Every Saturday *School House Rock* would come on during a commercial break and teach something about politics or grammar. One of their lessons was on conjunctions. They said words like *and* are conjunctions that join two words together. They used two train cars being held together by the word *and* to illustrate their point, which is what we have in verse 16. A person must believe *and* be baptized to be saved. Both these conditions must be met before salvation will occur.

We can prove this fact further by looking at the original Greek and its grammar. In our verse, *believe* and *is baptized* are aorist participles, and the word *and* is a coordinating conjunction that binds *believe* and *is baptized* together. Finally, our leading verb is *will be saved*. Basic Greek grammar states that an aorist participle's action occurs before the main verb, and in rare cases its action can occur at the same time of the main verb. Since *believe* and *is baptized* are joined by a coordinating conjunction, this means both *believe* and *is baptized* must take place before *will be saved* happens. This proves baptism is necessary to be saved. Please note the following comments made by Greek experts:

> The aorist participle denotes action prior to the action denoted by the leading verb, whether the action denoted by the leading

26

verb is past, present or future (Machen 116-117).

The time of action in participles is indicated in the relation of the action of the participle to the action of the main verb. The following indicates that relationship: The Aorist participle indicates action which is antecedent to the action of the main verb (Summers 89).

The Greek never used the aorist participle for subsequent action. "The aorist participle may suggest simultaneous action.... or antecedent action.... The Aorist participle never gives subsequent action.... No such example has ever been found (Robertson).

It is interesting that Mr. Robertson does not believe that baptism is necessary for salvation because of his theology, yet he understood the Greek grammar of the text demands it.

The aorist participle ... is antecedent to the time of the main verb, or sometimes coincidental with the time of the main verb (Mare).

In no case a thing subsequent to it, if all the rules of grammar and all sure understanding of language are not to be given up (Schmiedel).

Whether we examine the grammar of this text from the English or the Greek, we can see that both belief and baptism are necessary before a person can be saved.

Those who do not believe baptism is necessary do not like verse 16. So, they use two basic arguments to explain away the simplicity of it. Let's examine the first one. They say the second part of verse 16 shows that baptism is not necessary because it only says if a person does not believe, he will be condemned. Since Jesus did not include baptism in this statement, it means baptism is not necessary for salvation.

This is a desperate argument that does not have any merit because Jesus' last statement cannot negate what He just said. We can see this from the example used earlier. The announcer said: "If you will drive down to the Toyota dealership and be baptized you will receive a new car. If you do not drive down you will miss out on a new car." All the announcer had to say was: "If you do not drive down, then you will not get a new car." Everyone can understand that if a person does not drive down there, he is not going to get baptized.

We have the same situation with what Jesus said because if a person will not believe, he is not going to be baptized. So, that is all Jesus had to say. In fact, if a person does not believe, he will never do anything God has asked him to do, which is why Jesus said: "...he who does not believe is condemned already..." (Jn. 3:18). No matter how hard someone tries to change the simplicity of Jesus' words in our verse, it cannot be done.

Guy N. Woods said:

> This verse specifically declared that baptism is a part of God's plan to save today. Only as we yield our wills to the Lord, and only when we comply with His conditions are we promised pardon. Baptism, to a penitent believer, stands in relation to salvation as a condition precedent. Every reference to it in the New Testament either asserts or implies this connection. To appropriate the salvation Jesus offers to man, man must comply with the conditions

28

Jesus announced in this text. All the human ingenuity that can be brought to bear on this passage can never make it say and mean that he that believeth and is not baptized shall be saved (Woods, *Question and Answers*).

Since verse 16 cannot be explained away, their second argument is that this verse does not belong in the Bible. In fact, some scholars teach that verses 9 – 20 do not belong in the Gospel of Mark because they believe they were added at a later date, which would be a great argument for their side. If they can prove these verses do not belong there, then they do not have to worry about what it says.

Let's examine the most common arguments people use to justify removing verses 9 – 20. The most popular argument is found in many of our Bible versions, which comment on these verses in their notes.

ESV – Some manuscripts end the book with 16:8; others include verses 9-20 immediately after verse 8. A few manuscripts insert additional material after verse 14; one Latin manuscript adds after verse 8 the following: *But they reported briefly to Peter and those with him all that they had been told. And after this, Jesus himself sent out by means of them, from east to west, the sacred and imperishable proclamation of eternal salvation.* Other manuscripts include this same wording after verse 8, then continue with verses 9-20.

NRS – Some of the most ancient authorities bring the book to a close at the end of verse 8. One authority concludes the book with the shorter ending; others include the shorter ending and then continue with verses 9-20. In most authorities verses 9-20 follow immediately after verse 8, though in some of these authorities the passage is marked as being doubtful.

NKJ – Vv. 9-20 are bracketed in NU as not in the original text. They are lacking in Codex Sinaiticus and Codex Vaticanus, although nearly all other mss. of Mark contain them.

NIV – The most reliable early manuscripts and other ancient witnesses do not have Mark 16:9:20.

I could list more notes from other versions that say similar things, but these are enough to show the reason some would teach that these verses do not belong. The NIV and the NRS give the idea that the last twelve verses of Mark are not in the most reliable manuscripts, which is not a fair statement because it is misleading. It is important to understand that we do not have any of the original documents of the Bible from the first century. "The text of the New Testament is derived from three sources: Greek Manuscripts, Ancient Translations and Quotations from the Fathers" (Schaff). There is also another source that I will mention later.

We have approximately 5000 Greek Manuscripts that are copies of the original text, and they vary in age, content, and quality. The older the manuscript the more reliable it is supposed to be because it would be closer to the original date. However, this is not true in every case because it is possible that a later copy could have been copied from a source that had been copied fewer times than an earlier version. There are basically two types of Greek manuscripts. First, the Uncial manuscripts are dated around the 4th to the 10th century, and they are written in all capital letters. Second, the Minuscule manuscripts are dated around the 9th century and beyond, and they are written in lowercase and make up most of the manuscripts.

Since the Uncial manuscripts are the oldest, let's look at the five oldest manuscripts.

1. Codex Sinaiticus A (Aleph) – written around the 4th century.
2. Codex Vaticanius (Codex B) – written around the 4th century and is considered to be the most complete even though it does not contain 1 & 2 Timothy, Titus, Revelation, and part of Hebrews.
3. Codex Alexandrinus (Codex A) – written around the 5th century.
4. Codex Ephraemi Rescriptus (Codex C) – written around the 5th century.
5. Codex Bezae (Codex D) – written around the 6th century and only contains the Gospels and the book of Acts.

These first two manuscripts are what the NIV and NRS are calling the most ancient and reliable documents. It is true that neither one of these manuscripts contain the last twelve verses of Mark. However, Codex Vaticanius has a blank spot at the end of verse 8 that is big enough for the rest of the verses to be written. "Even the UBS Handbook admits that this suggests 'That the copyist of B knew of an ending but did not have it in the manuscript he was copying'" (Clarke 625).

The reason the statements of the NIV and NRS are misleading is because Codex A and C are only about 50 years later than these first two, and Codex D is around 100 years later. They are just as reliable as these first two, and all of them contain the last twelve verses of Mark. Out of these five oldest manuscripts, three contain the long ending. In fact, most of the manuscripts contain the long ending. Regarding the manuscripts that do not include the long ending, B.J. Clarke wrote: "Thomas proceeds to list the Greek manuscripts which end at Mark. 16:8: 'Aleph, B, 304 (2386 and 1420 have a page missing at this point)" (620). Notice the contrast. Only a few manuscripts stop at verse 8 compared to the hundreds of them that include these verses. The evidence from these manuscripts alone proves the long ending of Mark belongs there.

What about those two oldest manuscripts? Since they do not have the long ending, should we exclude those verses even though most of the other ones have it? The answer is no for several reasons. First, consider what Guy N. Woods said:

> Moreover, a little known fact is that included in the Sinaitic manuscript are apocryphal books with portions of Tobit, Ecclesiasticus, and other non-canonical writing. If the omission of Mark 16:9-20 from this document proves the passage to be spurious, does the inclusion of these apocryphal portions establish their reliability? (Woods, *Gospel Advocate*).

Mr. Woods is correct. If we are going to single out these two older manuscripts as our authority to remove the long ending of Mark, then we need to add these other apocryphal books to our Bibles. We also need to realize there are more verses that are missing from these two oldest manuscripts. B.J Clarke observed that:

> John 21:25 does not appear in either of these MSS. Does the NIV therefore separate this passage from the rest of John and provide an ominous explanatory note about its absence from the two most ancient manuscripts? No! ... Why? Because although John 21:25 is not found in Codex Sinaiticus and Codex Vaticanus, it is found in the overwhelming number of other manuscripts available to us, and

therefore has more than adequate attestation as a part of the New Testament text. The same thing is true about Mark 16:9-20 (625).

Here are a few more verses that are missing from either both or one of these two older manuscripts: Mark 1:1; Luke 6:1; 22:43; 23:34; John 9:38, 19:33-34; Ephesians 1:1; 1 & 2 Timothy; Titus; Hebrews 9:15 and the whole book of Revelation. Knowing these facts teaches us that we should base our conclusion on what the majority of the evidence says and not just two manuscripts.

Another important point is there are documents that are older than these two manuscripts that have the long ending of Mark. They come from our two other sources: ancient translations and quotations from the fathers. Again Mr. Woods writes:

> It should be observed that when it is said: "two of the oldest manuscripts of the New Testament omit it," this is far from being the same as saying the oldest copies of the New Testament are without it. These manuscripts are documents containing the text of New Testament Greek. The versions are translations into the language then in current use (Woods, *Gospel Advocate*).

He also said:

> The Old Syriac translation appeared and was in use in the shadow of the apostolic age – within the lifetime of many early Christians who could and did know John the apostle personally. Mark 16:9-20 is in this translation. Is also appears in the Ethiopic, Egyptian, Old Italic, Sahidic, and Coptic translations appear-

ing soon after the end of the first century, all much older than the two Greek manuscripts omitting it, evidencing the fact that the manuscript or manuscripts from which they were made all contained the segment. Two hundred years before the Vatican and Sinaitic manuscripts were copied, it was in the Scriptures then being used (Woods, *Gospel Advocate*).

Even though these are earlier writings that were translated into other languages, they came from the original Greek. Since they include the long ending of Mark, they prove it belongs there. Since the general rule is the closer a document is to the first century the more reliable it is, then these translations should be considered just as or more reliable than the Vatican and Sinaitic manuscripts.

Finally, the quotes from the early church fathers add more proof that Mark's long ending belongs there. It has been said that the entire New Testament except for eleven verses could be reconstructed from the writing of the early church fathers. They quoted verses from the long ending of Mark, and here is a list of the ones that do:

Second century:

- Irenaeus
- Papias
- Justin Martyr

Third century:

- Hyppolytus
- Celsus

Fourth century:

- Aphreates

- Cyril of Jerusalem
- Ephipanus
- Ambrose
- Chrysostom
- Augustine

Out all these early church fathers Irenaeus is the most significant because he was a pupil of Polycarp who was a companion to the apostles and a pupil of John. So, writing around A.D. 180 he confirmed the long ending of Mark.

Earlier, I mentioned there was another source. That source comes from Lectionaries. These were manuscripts containing selected passages of Scriptures that would be read in pubic worship services. There are around 2000 of them with some of them possibly dating to the 4th century or earlier. Burgon said: "All the twelve verses in dispute are found in every known copy of the venerable Lectionary of the East" (Burgon).

All the evidence I have provided proves the long ending of Mark should be there, and no other arguments can disprove it. For instance, some argue that the style and many of the words in the last 12 verses are different then the rest of Mark's account.

B.J. Clarke notes:

> One of the best demonstrations of how frail the vocabulary argument is comes for the pen of J. W. McGarvey. He reported that he examined the last twelve verses of Luke's Gospel and found nine words which are not elsewhere used in his narrative, and among them are four which are not elsewhere used in his

narrative, and among them are four which are not elsewhere found in the New Testament. He writes that

>...none of our critics have thought it worthwhile to mention this fact, if they have noticed it, much less have they raised a doubt in regard to the genuineness of this passage. Doubtless many other examples of the same kind could be found in the New Testament; but these are amply sufficient to show that the argument, which we are considering is but a shallow sophism.

>McGarvey also pointed out that the change of subject matter at the end justified the use of different words. Further, he noted that though some of the words in 16:9-20 were not used in their simple forms in the Gospel, they were nonetheless constantly used in composition with prepositions (644).

Others have claimed that Eusebius (A.D. 330) and Jerome (A.D. 420) said that the long ending did not belong there. First, Jerome was just repeating what Eusibius said. Second, Eusebius did not say that he believed the long ending should not be there, but that some might not think that it belongs there. The reason for this assessment was that during his time there were some copies of Mark that did not have the long ending. However, the evidence I have presented, especially from Irenaeus who wrote 150 years before Eusebius, proves that the long ending should be there.

It would be strange for Mark to end his Gospel at verse eight with the women being afraid. Those who argue against the long ending recognize this point, and they offer various reasons why the book ended abruptly. Some suggest Mark may have died before he was able to finish his book, or maybe he intended to write another volume like Luke did. Many other speculations have been made, but they are just that, speculations. For a more in-depth look at this topic, I recommend B.J. Clarke's article, "Does Mark 16:9-20 Belong in the Bible" (615-660).

In conclusion, it amazes me how far some will go to disprove the necessity of baptism. We have examined two of the most common arguments used against Mark 16:16, and I have shown these arguments are just a desperate attempt to avoid the simple message that a person must believe and be baptized to be saved.

Questions

1. How does the grammar from the English and Greek prove we must believe and be baptized to be saved?
2. Since Jesus taught that those who do not believe will be condemned, does this mean baptism is not necessary? Why or why not?
3. Discuss the internal and external evidence that proves the long ending of Mark belongs in the Bible.

THE BEGINNING OF THE CHURCH
Acts 2:38

4

Acts 2 records one of the most important events in human history because it marks the birth of church, and it proves that Jesus is the Messiah. Before we look at verse 38, let us briefly consider the significance of this chapter. God has always had a master plan to save humankind from their sins, and that plan involved the coming of the Messiah. We get our first glimpse of this plan in Genesis 3:15. There are over 300 prophecies throughout the Old Testament about the coming Messiah, which describe where He would be born, how He would live His life, and how He would die. Jesus fulfilled all the prophecies written about His work on the earth (Lk. 24:44; Jn. 17:4). Since He fulfilled hundreds of prophecies, which included many things He would have no control over, such as where He was born (Mic. 5:2), the casting of lots for His clothing (Ps. 22:18), and none of His bones being broken (Ps. 34:20) offers overwhelming proof that He is the Messiah.

The fulfillment of these prophecies would be meaningless if Jesus had not been raised from the dead (1 Cor. 15:12-19) or if He did not keep His promise of sending the Holy Spirit to His apostles (Lk. 24:49; Jn. 16:5-15; Acts 1:8). Acts 2 shows the fulfillment of Jesus' promise (Acts 2:1-4), which proves that He was sitting at the right hand of God (Acts 2:33).

Further proof that the apostles had received the promise of the Holy Spirit and that Jesus was raised from the dead can be found in their attitude change. When Jesus' apostles were with Him, they were unorganized, divided, and concerned about who would be the greatest in the kingdom (Mk. 10:41; Lk. 22:24). After Jesus was crucified His apostles were scared, and they were hiding from the Jews (Jn. 20:19). However, when the day of Pentecost came, the apostles were no longer fearful, and they boldly proclaimed Jesus' death, burial, and resurrection to thousands of Jews. From that point forward, these men were united, and they knew exactly what to do (Acts 4:13). They were no longer worried about their life, which can be seen in their bold statements such as: "Whether it is right in the sight of God to listen to you more than to God, you judge. For we cannot but speak the things which we have seen and heard" (Acts 4:19-20). Their sudden attitude change and ability to know what to say and do proves Jesus was the Messiah, and it proves He sent the Holy Spirit of promise to them.

Acts 2 also records the birth of the church and the beginning of God's kingdom. First, we need to realize that the church and the kingdom are referring to the same thing. There is a lot of confusion in the religious world on this simple concept because many teach that instead of receiving the kingdom like we should have, we were given the church instead. When people say this, whether they realize it our not, they are saying that Jesus failed His mission, and the Old Testament prophecies were wrong.

To show that the kingdom and the church are the same, consider the following:

- The kingdom and the church are entered the same way (Jn. 3:3-5; Acts 2:38, 41, 47; 1 Cor 12:13).
- The word *church* and *kingdom* are used interchangeably (Mt. 16:18-19; Heb. 12:22-24, 28).

- Daniel prophesied that the kingdom would begin during the Roman Empire (Dan. 2:31-45).
- Isaiah said the kingdom would begin in the last days at Jerusalem (Isa. 2:1-3), which is what we see happening in Acts 2 because Peter said this event was happening in the last days (Acts 2:14-21).
- While Jesus was on the earth, both John and Jesus spoke of the kingdom as being at hand (Mt. 3:1-3; 4:17; 6:9; 10:7). However, after the day of Pentecost, the kingdom is spoken of as a present reality (Col. 1:13; Acts 8:12; Rev. 1:9).
- Jesus said the kingdom would come with power (Mk. 9:1), and the Spirit and the power would come together (Lk. 24:44-49). So, when the spirit came on the day of Pentecost, the kingdom came with power.

All these points prove that the church and the kingdom are interchangeable terms, and Acts 2 marks the beginning of the church/kingdom.

These events occurred on the day of Pentecost, which means fiftieth. Pentecost or Feast of Weeks (Num. 18:26; Lev. 23:17) was a Jewish festival to give thanks for the harvest and a time to offer their first fruits to God (Ex. 23:16; Num. 28:26). Pentecost happened 50 days after the Sabbath of the Passover week, which always occurred on the first day of the week (Lev. 23:15-16). So, the birth of the church happened on the first day of the week. This became a special day to the Christian because Jesus was raised from the dead on the first day of the week (Mk. 16:9), the church began that day, and we are commanded to give (1 Cor. 16:2) and partake of the Lord's Supper that day (Acts 20:7). This is the reason we assemble to worship God on the first day of every week.

After the apostles finished boldly preaching Jesus' death, burial, and resurrection many of the Jews were pricked in their heart, which caused them to ask one of the most important questions that any human could ask, "Men and brethren, what shall we do?" (Acts 2:37). When we learn about the love of God, what He did for us, and how we are nothing without Him, we should all want to know what we must do to be saved. Notice Peter's response:

Then Peter said to them, "Repent, and let every one of you be baptized in the name of Jesus Christ for the remission of sins; and you shall receive the gift of the Holy Spirit. "For the promise is to you and to your children, and to all who are afar off, as many as the Lord our God will call." And with many other words he testified and exhorted them, saying, "Be saved from this perverse generation." Then those who gladly received his word were baptized; and that day about three thousand souls were added *to them.* And they continued steadfastly in the apostles' doctrine and fellowship, in the breaking of bread, and in prayers (Acts 2:38-42).

I am confident that if a person would read what Peter has said without any preconceived ideas, he would understand that a person must repent and be baptized in the name of Jesus Christ for the remission of sins. Peter clearly teaches that we must repent and be baptized before we will receive the forgiveness of our sin or the gift of the Holy Spirit. However, those who teach we are saved by faith alone, or that baptism is not necessary, have to find a way to make this passage teach something different, which is sad, but true.

Before we examine the objections that some have invented to take baptism out of the plan of salvation, let's examine our text in more detail. The Jews who asked this question were believers in Jesus because they had heard the truth, and it convicted them. However, their belief was not enough or else Peter would have told them they had nothing else to do if they were already saved. This fact alone proves we are not saved by faith alone (also see James 2:14-26). Peter told them they needed to repent. *Repent* means: "To change one's mind for better, heartily to amend with abhorrence of one's past sins" (Thayer). Repenting does not mean that a person is just sorry for getting caught at his sin. Instead, it means a person is convicted by his sin, and he is going to make a change in his life and do his best not to engage in that sin again.

Peter does not stop there; he adds another step with the word *and*. Not only are they to repent, they must also be baptized in the name of Jesus, which was a command they could follow. They could repent, and they could be baptized, which refers to water baptism. When Peter said, "in the name of Jesus Christ," he was not giving a word formula that must be said when we are baptized. Instead, he is saying that we must be baptized by the authority of Christ. If it is not done by His authority, then we are just getting wet because we do not understand the reason we are being baptized. As I pointed out in the chapter on The Great Commission, when we are baptized into Christ, we are baptized into the possession or care of the Godhead, which is why we need to understand the reason we are being baptized.

Some religious groups believe we are supposed to say some specific words at a person's baptism, but the Bible does not give one example of what anyone said as someone was being baptized. Therefore, as long as a person knows he is being baptized by the authority of Jesus, no words have to be spoken. When I assist someone in their baptism, I will usually say: "You are being baptized in the name of the Father, the Son, and the Holy Spirit for the remission of your sins." However, I do not say this as a word formula. I only say it for the benefit of the people that are observing the baptism so they will know the reason that person is being baptized and by whose authority.

Peter said that baptism is for the remission of sins. Remember, repentance is linked with baptism by the conjunction *and*, which means both of these must occur before remission of sins will happen. *Remission* means: "Forgiveness or pardon, of sins" (Thayer). Obviously, we cannot be saved or even hope to enter heaven unless our sins have been forgiven. Therefore, if we just believe in Jesus, we are not saved because our sins have not been forgiven. If we just believe and repent, our sins are still with us. However, if we believe, repent, and are baptized, then our sins will be removed as the apostle Paul found out (Acts 22:16). Although not mentioned in this text, we also know that we must confess Jesus as our Lord to be saved as well (Rom. 10:9-10). However, baptism is the point at which our sins are removed (Acts 2:38; 22:16), and we contact the blood of Jesus (Rev. 1:5).

Finally, Peter used the conjunction *and* to show that we receive the gift of the Holy Spirit when we receive the remission of our sins, which means we have been sealed by Him (Eph. 1:13; 4:30; 2 Cor. 1:22). For more information on the gift of the Holy Spirit, see my chapter on John 3:3-5. So, without repentance and baptism, we cannot have the forgiveness of our sins or the gift of the Holy Spirit.

Peter continued preaching and exhorting these Jews, telling them to be saved from this perverse generation. Many of those listening that day were ready to be saved, and they were saved when they gladly received his message and were baptized for the remission of their sins. About 3000 souls were added to the church/kingdom that day by God (Acts 2:47; Jn. 3:3-5).

Peter's message is easy to understand. If people would read Peter's message with an open unbiased heart, they would all realize that repentance and baptism are necessary for salvation.

In this last section, I will deal with all the objections of Acts 2:38 that some use to teach that baptism has nothing to do with our salvation. The first objection comes from the Greek word *eis*, which means "into, unto, to, towards, for, among" (Thayer). Some teach that this word could mean *because of* in certain instances. So they have Peter saying that we should repent and be baptized *because of* the remission of sins, which makes baptism something we do after our sins have already been forgiven. However, they want us to believe that repentance must be done before the remission of sins, which cannot be because whatever repentance is for, so is baptism. We cannot separate these two because they are joined by the coordinating conjunction *and*. So, if baptism is something we do because we have already obtained the forgiveness of sin, then repentance is also something we do after the forgiveness of our sins.

The Greek word *eis* is used over 2000 times in the New Testament and it is never translated as *because of*. Let's examine a verse that is worded similar to Acts 2:38.

"For this is My blood of the new covenant, which is shed for many <u>for</u> the remission of sins" (Mt. 26:28).

Notice, Jesus shed His blood for *eis* the remission of sins. If we render *eis* as *because of*, then Jesus shed His blood because the remission of sins was already in place. No one would dream of changing the meaning of this verse, but they have no problem changing the meaning of Acts 2:38. For instance, A.T. Robertson, a Baptist scholar, had no problem understanding what *eis* meant in Mt. 26:28:

> He had the definite conception of his death on the cross as the basis of forgiveness of sin. The purpose of the shedding of his blood of the New Covenant was precisely to remove (forgive) sins (Robertson).

45

However when it came to Acts 2:38, notice what he said:

> Unto the remission of your sins (*eis aphesin tôn hamartiôn hûmôn*). This phrase is the subject of endless controversy as men look at it from the standpoint of sacramental or of evangelical theology... One will decide the use here according as he believes that baptism is essential to the remission of sins or not. My view is decidedly against the idea that Peter, Paul, or any one in the New Testament taught baptism as essential to the remission of sins or the means of securing such remission. So I understand Peter to be urging baptism on each of them who had already turned (repented) and for it to be done in the name of Jesus Christ on the basis of the forgiveness of sins which they had already received (Robertson).

He is saying, instead of relying on the grammar of this verse, or the meaning of the word *eis*, we have to decide what it means based on our theology whether baptism is for or because of the remission of sins. Mr. Robertson also associates repentance with turning to the Lord, but this is not the case. To prove my point, I want to show that turning to the Lord is equivalent to being saved and added to the Lord.

And the hand of the Lord was with them, and a great number <u>believed and turned to the Lord</u>. Then news of these things came to the ears of the church in Jerusalem, and they sent out Barnabas to go as far as Antioch. When he came and had seen the grace of God, he was glad, and encouraged them all that with purpose of heart they should continue with the Lord. For he was a good man, full of the Holy Spirit and of faith. And a great many people were <u>added to the Lord</u> (Acts 11:21).

When the Christians spread out because of Stephen's death, they went out and successfully proclaimed God's Word everywhere they went. Luke teaches that a great number believed and turned to the Lord. In the last part of this passage, we can see that turning to the Lord is equivalent to being added to the Lord. However, the word *believed* is an aorist participle, which means it takes place before the main verb *turned*. These verses show that turning to the Lord is equal to being saved, and belief happens before one turns to the Lord, which clearly shows that something more than belief must occur before one can be saved.

But declared first to those in Damascus, then in Jerusalem and throughout all the region of Judea, and also to the Gentiles, that they <u>should repent and turn to God,</u> performing deeds in keeping with their repentance (Acts 26:20, ESV).

Notice, they had to repent and turn to God, which means that repentance is something different than turning to God. We have learned that both belief and repentance are not equivalent to turning to the Lord. So, when does a person turn to the Lord? We can find out by comparing Acts 2:38 to Acts 3:19.

"<u>Repent,</u> and let every one of you <u>be baptized in the name of Jesus Christ for the remission of sins</u>; and you shall <u>receive the gift of the Holy Spirit</u>" (Acts 2:38).

"<u>Repent</u> therefore, and <u>turn again, that your sins may be blotted out,</u> that <u>times of refreshing may come from the presence of the Lord,</u> and that he may send the Christ appointed for you, Jesus" (Acts 3:19-20, ESV).

In this last passage, Peter was teaching the same message he did on the day of Pentecost. We can see that *turn again* happens after repentance, and as we compare these two passages, it becomes clear that *turn again, that your sins may be blotted out* is equivalent to *be baptized … for the remission of sins.* This proves that baptism is for the remission of sins. Also, *receive the gift of the Holy Spirit* is equivalent to *times of refreshing.*

Another argument people use to change the meaning of *eis* to *because of* in our passage is by saying there are four or five places the word *eis* would make more sense to translate as *because o"* However, these four or five places they refer to are controversial, and it can be shown how the standard translations of *eis* can be used. But, let's say they are right and there are four or five places that *eis* could be translated *because of.* This would mean out of the 2000 + times *eis* is used, only four or five instances meant *because of.* Therefore, using *because of* would be rare and something in the text would have to demand that *eis* be translated to *because of.*

Is there anything in Acts 2:38 that would demand such a translation? No! To put this argument to rest, consider the following points.

First, repentance and baptism are tied together by the coordinating conjunction *and*, which means if baptism is because of the remission of sins, so is repentance.

Second, when we examine the whole counsel of God, we will learn that baptism washes away our sins (Acts 22:16; 1 Cor. 6:11), puts us into Christ (Gal. 3:27; Rom. 6:3), and saves us (1 Pet. 3:21). While more verses could be used, these are sufficient to show there are no exceptions in Acts 2:38 to justify changing *eis* to *because of* because baptism is for the remission of sins. So, even if we allow them to have their four or five exceptions, it still does not help them with Acts 2:38.

Another Greek argument made against baptism in Acts 2:38 is that the words *repent* and *be baptized* are different in person and number. Specifically, *repent* is 2nd person plural and *be bap-*

tized is 3rd person singular. Therefore, they claim the phrase *for the remission of sin* cannot refer to both verbs. Of course they chose baptism as being the one that must be excluded. When people have to go to extremes like this to explain away clear passages, it should cause us to raise an eyebrow. However, there is no truth to this argument, and I can prove this by the following quotes from two different authors who examined this argument.

> In early 1968, I wrote a letter to F.W. Gingrich, co-translator of the famous Arndt-Gingrich *Greek-English Lexicon of the New Testament* and *Other Early Christians Literature*. The letter, dated February 12, 1968, reads as follows:
>
> "Dear Professor Gingrich: Is it grammatically possible that the phrase 'for the remission of sins,' in Acts 2:38, expresses the force of both verbs, 'repent ye' and 'be baptized each one of you,' even though these verbs differ in both person and number?"
>
> From Albright College, Reading, Pennsylvania (February 21, 1968), Gingrich replied:
>
> "Yes. The difference between *metanoesate* (repent) and *baptistheto* (be baptized) is simply that in the first, the people are viewed together in the plural, while the second the emphasis is on each individual (Jackson, *The Acts of the Apostles* 28).

David Padfield wrote to four different Greek scholars and asked them the following question:

Is it grammatically possible that the phrase 'eis aphesin hamartion,' 'for the remission of sins,' as used in Acts 2:38, expresses the force of both verbs, 'repent ye and be baptized each one of you,' even though these verbs differ in both person and number?"

Their response is as follows:

1. Bruce Metzger wrote: "In reply to your recent inquiry may I say that, in my view, the phrase 'eis aphesin hamartion' in Acts 2:38 applies to both of the preceding verbs."

2. F.W. Gingrich wrote: "The difference in person and number of 'repent' and 'be baptized' is caused by the fact that 'repent' is a direct address in the second person plural, while 'be baptized' is governed by the subject 'every one of you' and so is third person singular. 'Every one of you' is, of course, a collective noun."

3. Arthur L. Farstad wrote: "Since the expression 'eis aphesin hamartion' is a prepositional phrase with no verbal endings or singular or plural endings. I certainly agree that grammatically it can go with both repentance and baptism. In fact, I would think that it does go with both of them."

4. John R. Werner wrote, Whenever two verbs are connected by kai 'and' and then followed by a modifier (such as a prepositional phrase, as in Acts 2:38), it is grammatically possible that modifier modifies either both the verbs, or the latter one. This is because there is no punctuation in the ancient manuscripts, so we don't know whether the author intended to pause between the first verb and the 'and.' It

50

does not matter that, here in Acts 2:38, one of the verbs is second person plural ("y'all") and the other is third-person singular ("is to"). They are both imperative, and the fact that they are joined by kai 'and' is sufficient evidence that the author may have regarded them as a single unit to which his modifier applied (Padfield).

The quotes from these Greek scholars prove that this invented Greek argument against baptism has no merit, and it is just another desperate attempt to twist a clear passage and make it fit with their doctrine.

The final argument I want to examine comes from those who teach that sprinkling or pouring is an acceptable mode of baptism. They claim there was not enough time or water to baptize 3000 people there, so they must have sprinkled water on them or poured water on them.

First, this does not agree with the meaning of *baptism*, which means to dip or immerse.

Second, there was plenty of time to baptize 3000 people. Peter started preaching around 9 A.M., and even if he did not finish until noon, there was still be plenty of time. It is possible to baptize one person every minute, and there were twelve apostles. They could have baptized all these people in about four and a half hours, which does not include the possibility of the new Christians helping with the baptisms.

Third, as far as having enough water available, archeologists have proven there was plenty of water available close to the temple. The pool of Siloam (immediately south of the Temple enclosure) is still used today for the immersion of believers (Reese 81).

Note what McGarvey said:

> As to the quantity of available water, Dr. J. T. Barclay, in his work entitled "The City of the Great King," written during a residence of three years and a half in Jerusalem, as a missionary, shows that Jerusalem was anciently better supplied with water than any other city known to history not permeated by living streams. Even to the present day, though most of the public reservoirs are now dry, such as the supposed pool of Bethesda, 365 feet long by 131 in breadth, and the lower pool of Gihon, 600 long by 260 in breadth, there are still in existence bodies of water, such as the pool of Siloam, and the pool of Hezekiah, affording most ample facilities for immersing any number of persons (McGarvey).

These three points prove there was plenty of water and time to baptized 3000 people, which does not leave any room for the false doctrine of sprinkling or pouring.

In conclusion, we have learned that Acts 2 records one of the greatest events in the history of humankind. We have learned that we must repent and be baptized before we can receive the remission of our sins or the gift of the Holy Spirit. We examined several opposing Greek arguments and we learned they did not have any merit. Finally, I proved there was enough water and time to baptize 3000 people on that day.

Questions

1. Discuss the significance of Acts 2.
2. How can we prove that the church and the kingdom are the same thing?
3. Why is the first day of the week important?
4. What did Peter say was necessary for the remission of sins?
5. Discuss the various arguments people use against Acts 2:38.

CONVERSIONS BY PHILIP
THE EVANGELIST
ACTS 8

5

After Stephen's death a great persecution arose against the church, and the disciples of Christ were scattered throughout Judea and Samaria, but the apostles remained in Jerusalem (Acts 8:1). Saul was doing his part to wreak havoc on the church as he drug both men and women to prison (Acts 8:3). Men like Saul thought they could destroy this new movement, but all they did was help it grow because it caused these disciples to go to new areas and preach the good news about Jesus (Acts 8:4), which is exactly what Jesus wanted. He told His disciples: "But you shall receive power when the Holy Spirit has come upon you; and you shall be witnesses to Me in Jerusalem, and in all Judea and Samaria, and to the end of the earth" (Acts 1:8).

Many unnamed disciples went out and preached the Word, but Luke records the work of Philip the evangelist. This is the same Philip who was chosen to be one of the seven men who took care of a problem that had developed over the Grecian widows (Acts 6). These seven men are the first recorded to have the apostles lay their hands on them so they could receive the miraculous gifts of the Holy Spirit.

Then Philip went down to the city of Samaria and preached Christ to them. And the multitudes with one accord heeded the things spoken by Philip, hearing and seeing the miracles which he did. For unclean spirits, crying with a loud voice, came out of many who were possessed; and many who were paralyzed and lame were healed. And there was great joy in that city (Acts 8:5-8).

The city of Samaria was located in the country of Samaria, north of Jerusalem, and it was at a lower elevation than Jerusalem, which is why Luke wrote, "Philip went down to the city." For Philip to go to Samaria and preach the Word, he had to overcome the typical prejudice against these people. Most full-blooded Jews would not enter Samaria because they were considered an impure race. Samaritans were part Jew and part Gentile. The rabbis prohibited Judean Jews from setting foot on Samaritan territory because it would make them unclean according to the Babylonian Talmud. There was not much love between these two groups. To help us understand the reason the full-blooded Jews despised the Samaritans, let's take a closer look at their origin and how this all began.

The territory of Samaria was comprised of two tribes - Ephraim and part of Manasseh. After the children of Israel divided into two kingdoms, King Omri started building the city of Samaria around 880 B.C. His son Ahab finished its construction around 874 – 853 B.C. This city became the capital of Israel. Due to Israel's constant disobedience to God, the Assyrians captured their capital around 722 – 721 B.C., and many of the Israelites were taken away to Assyria (2 Kgs. 17:23). Next, Assyria took over the city of Samaria, and they brought in various foreigners (2 Kgs. 17:24). Not all the Israelites were taken because some were left to work the vineyards and fields, while others escaped (2 Chr. 30:6). These foreigners would eventually marry these Israelites and each other, and that is where the Samaritans came from (2 Kgs. 17:29).

They were called Samaritans because they occupied Samaria. Mixing these different nationalities was a strategy the Assyrians used to cause them to lose their identity so they would be less of a threat to the Assyrians in the future. It is important to remember that it was against God's Law for Jews to marry foreigners, but they did it anyway. Once these mixed people were living in Samaria, God sent lions to eat some of them because they did not fear God (2 Kgs. 17:25). They wanted to appease God, so they sent for a priest to teach them the ways of God. From that point forward, they worshipped God, but they also continued worshipping their false gods (2 Kgs. 17:26ff).

Later, Judah was captured by the Babylonians, and 70 years later they began to come back to their homeland. The Samaritans offered to help Zerubbabel rebuild the temple, but he refused their help. This made the Samaritans angry; so they tried to prevent the Jews from rebuilding the temple (Ezra 4:1-10). They also tried to prevent Nehemiah from rebuilding the wall of Jerusalem (Neh. 2:10 – 6:14). When Ezra commanded the Jews to divorce their pagan wives (Ezra 9 – 11), it divided the Jews from the Samaritans even more. According to Josephus, the final event that would forever separate the Jews from the Samaritans was when they built a temple on Mount Gerizim (Josephus, *The Antiquities of the Jews* xi, vii, 2; viii, 2 ff). They claimed this area, known as Shechem, as being the true *Bethel* (house of God) instead of Jerusalem (Nelson New Illustrated Bible Dictionary 1120).

At some point, the Samaritans put away their pagan gods, and they regulated their worship by the Torah. They believed the first five books of the Bible were God's Word, but they did not recognize any of the other books in the Old Testament as being from God.

Philip overcame this typical prejudice, and he preached the soul saving message of Jesus to the Samaritans. To prove his message was from God, he worked signs and miracles. Some of them were possessed by demons, so he cast them out. Others were paralyzed and lame, so he healed them. Luke tells us that these people rejoiced. They had a lot to be joyful about because, not only did they hear the words that would save their soul, they were being healed, and the demons were being driven away.

But there was a certain man called Simon, who previously practiced sorcery in the city and astonished the people of Samaria, claiming that he was someone great, to whom they all gave heed, from the least to the greatest, saying, "This man is the great power of God." And they heeded him because he had astonished them with his sorceries for a long time. But when they believed Philip as he preached the things concerning the kingdom of God and the name of Jesus Christ, both men and women were baptized. Then Simon himself also believed; and when he was baptized he continued with Philip, and was amazed, seeing the miracles and signs which were done (Acts 8:9-13).

Simon was a common name during the first century. The early *church fathers* wrote many speculative things about this man, but I am mainly concerned about what Luke writes about him. We learn that Simon practiced magic, and he was obviously good at it since he had the Samaritans eating out of his hands. He used his fake magic to take advantage of these people, and they called him *the great power of God*.

> According to Irenaeus, Simon claimed to combine in himself the three persons of the trinity, alleging that he appeared to the Jews as the Son, to the Samaritans as the Father, and among the Gentiles as the Holy Spirit (Against Heresies, I. 23. 1 [Reese.320]).

Even though Simon was good at his fake magic, it failed in comparison to the real miracles and signs Philip was doing by the power of God. Philip's miracles caused them to stop listening to Simon and to start listening to Philip as he preached the good news about the kingdom of God and about the name of Jesus. Philip was preaching the same basic message that every other disciple of Christ was preaching, which would have been similar to the message taught by the apostles on the day of Pentecost. Even though we do not know the exact message he preached, we can know that he taught them about the necessity of baptism because men and women were baptized after hearing his message. Even Simon believed and obeyed the gospel by being baptized. Simon continued to be amazed by the real miracles and signs that were being done by Philip.

Now when the apostles who were at Jerusalem heard that Samaria had received the word of God, they sent Peter and John to them, who, when they had come down, prayed for them that they might receive the Holy Spirit. For as yet He had fallen upon none of them. They had only been baptized in the name of the Lord Jesus. Then they laid hands on them, and they received the Holy Spirit (Acts 8:14-17).

The Samaritans had received the implanted Word, which was able to save their souls (Jam. 1:21), just as the Jews did on the day of Pentecost. "Then those who gladly received his word were baptized; and that day about three thousand souls were added *to them*" (Acts 2:41). Therefore, receiving the Word of God, which saves a person, includes baptism.

When this news came to Jerusalem about the Samaritans, the apostles sent Peter and John. Please note, Peter was not serving as the head of the church or giving out orders. Instead, he was sent with John by the unanimous decision of the apostles. One can only wonder if John recalled the time he was ready to call down fire on a Samaritan Village (Lk. 9:54).

The reason these two apostles were sent was so they could bestow the miraculous gifts of the Holy Spirit on the Samaritans by the laying on of their hands. Only the apostles had this ability (2 Cor. 12:12), which is why Paul told the Romans: "For I long to see you, that I may impart to you some spiritual gift, so that you may be established" (Rom. 1:11). If others could have imparted spiritual gifts, there would be no need for Paul to go to Rome. Also, if it were possible for Philip to impart the miraculous gifts of the Holy Spirit on the Samaritans, then Peter and John could have stayed in Jerusalem. This fact proves that Luke was talking about receiving the miraculous gifts of the Holy Spirit and not the indwelling of the Holy Spirit that every Christian receives when they are baptized (Acts 2:38-39). We can also know this is not talking about Holy Spirit baptism, which happened on the day of Pentecost and to Cornelius's household because it did not require the laying on of hands. Since only the apostles could pass on the miraculous gifts, this means that miracles and signs would no longer be possible after the last apostle died. Also, Paul teaches us that miracles and signs would be done away with once the Word of God was fully revealed (1 Cor. 13:8-13).

Understanding this truth is important because it proves that these Samaritans were saved by obeying the gospel, which included being baptized in water in the name of Jesus. Their salvation was not dependent on them receiving the miraculous gifts of the Holy Spirit or Holy Spirit baptism as some teach. If someone claims the one baptism that saves (Eph. 4:5) is Holy Spirit baptism, then we have Philip, who was inspired by the Holy Spirit, coming to Samaria, preaching to them, baptizing them in water, and then leaving them in a lost state since they had not yet received the Holy Spirit. Would that make any sense? Of course not! Philip taught them and baptized them for the remission of their sins just as Jesus commanded His disciples to do (Mt. 28:19; Mk. 16:16).

And when Simon saw that through the laying on of the apostles' hands the Holy Spirit was given, he offered them money, saying, "Give me this power also, that anyone on whom I lay hands may receive the Holy Spirit." But Peter said to him, "Your money perish with you, because you thought that the gift of God could be purchased with money! You have neither part nor portion in this matter, for your heart is not right in the sight of God. Repent therefore of this your wickedness, and pray God if perhaps the thought of your heart may be forgiven you. For I see that you are poisoned by bitterness and bound by iniquity." Then Simon answered and said, "Pray to the Lord for me, that none of the things which you have spoken may come upon me" (Acts 8:18-24).

These passages show how quickly someone can be saved, fall away, and be restored. Simon saw how the apostles could pass on the miraculous gifts of the Holy Spirit, and he wanted that ability. In his previous work as a magician, it was a common practice for the squire to pay his teacher to acquire more magic tricks. Simon had turned his mind back to his worldly ways, and he wanted to purchase this ability. His actions that day caused a new word to be created.

> Simony - The buying or selling of ecclesiastical pardons, offices, or emoluments. [Middle English simonie, from Old French, from Late Latin simōnia, after Simon Magus, a sorcerer who tried to buy spiritual powers from the Apostle Peter (Acts 8:9-24)] (*American Heritage Dictionary*).

Peter quickly condemned Simon's sin with some strong words and commanded him to repent. The ability to pass on the miraculous gifts could only be done by the apostles, and no one could purchase this ability because it was a gift from God. Our text does not specifically say he repented, but it is implied because he asked Peter to pray for him. Another lesson learned here is that a person only has to be baptized one time the right way. After a person becomes a child of God, all he has to do is repent and confess his sins to God, and those sins will be forgiven (1 Jn. 1:9). Next, we learn about another conversion by Philip.

Now an angel of the Lord spoke to Philip, saying, "Arise and go toward the south along the road which goes down from Jerusalem to Gaza." This is desert (Acts 8:26).

God used an angel to direct Philip to the right location to meet a man who was ready to hear the gospel. Angels are used in many different ways, but they were never used to proclaim the gospel to the lost (Acts 11:13-14). He is told to go south toward the road that goes between Jerusalem and Gaza. Gaza is one of the oldest places mentioned in the Bible (Gen. 10:19). Some get confused with the term *desert* because they think of a place where there is no life or water. However, McGarvey notes:

> The term desert is not here to be understood in its stricter sense of a barren waste, but in its more general acceptation, of a place thinly inhabited. Such an interpretation is required by the geography of the country, and by the fact that water was found for the immersion of the eunuch. The only road from Jerusalem to Gaza, which passed through a level district suitable for wheeled vehicles, was that by Bethlehem to Hebron, and thence across a

plain to Gaza. According to Dr. Hackett, this is "the desert" of Luke 1:80, in which John the Immerser grew up. Dr. S. T. Barclay, who traversed this entire route in May, 1853, says that he traveled, after leaving "the immediate vicinity of Hebron, over one of the very best roads (with slight exceptions) and one of the most fertile countries that I ever beheld." [*City of the Great King*, p. 576.] (McGarvey).

So he arose and went. And behold, a man of Ethiopia, a eunuch of great authority under Candace the queen of the Ethiopians, who had charge of all her treasury, and had come to Jerusalem to worship, was returning. And sitting in his chariot, he was reading Isaiah the prophet (Acts 8:27-28).

Philip does not argue with the angel, he arose and went. We have no way of knowing if this eunuch was a Jew or a proselyte. However, we do know that he was a treasurer of one of the Queens of Ethiopia. All the Queens of Ethiopia were called Candace, which is similar to how the rulers of Egypt were called Pharaoh, and the rulers of Rome were called Caesar.

According to the BDAG Lexicon, eunuchs were: "A castrated male person … Eunuchs served, esp. in the orient, as keepers of a harem (Esth. 2:14) and not infreq. rose to high positions in the state." Even though this eunuch was not allowed to go into the temple, he still traveled hundreds of miles to worship God in Jerusalem, which shows how dedicated he was. I wish more Christians today had the same zeal to worship God as this eunuch did. He was returning home on his chariot and reading a scroll from Isaiah the prophet out loud.

Then the Spirit said to Philip, "Go near and overtake this chariot." So Philip ran to him, and heard him reading the prophet Isaiah, and said, "Do you understand what you are reading?" And he said, "How can I, unless someone guides me?" And he asked Philip to come up and sit with him (Acts 8:29-31).

First, the angel directed Philip toward the road, and now the Holy Spirit was telling him to go and overtake the eunuch's chariot. Just as the angels did not teach the lost the gospel, the Holy Spirit does not do it either. Instead, He would direct preachers like Philip to the person that needed to hear it.

Philip hears the eunuch reading from Isaiah, and he asked him a great question, "Do you understand what you are reading?" A person could read all kinds of things, but if he does not understand it, it will not be useful to him. The eunuch did not understand what he was reading, and he needed someone to guide him or explain it to him. His lack of understanding does not mean that we cannot read and understand the Scriptures on our own because we can (Acts 17:11; Eph. 3:3-5; 1 Pet. 2:2; 2 Pet. 1:19; Rev. 1:3). However, sometimes a person new to reading the Bible can benefit from a person who has studied it for years. So, the eunuch invited Philip to join him.

The place in the Scripture which he read was this: "He was led as a sheep to the slaughter; And as a lamb before its shearer *is* silent, So He opened not His mouth. In His humiliation His justice was taken away, And who will declare His generation? For His life is taken from the earth." So the eunuch answered Philip and said, "I ask you, of whom does the prophet say this, of himself or of some other man?" Then Philip opened his mouth, and beginning at this Scripture, preached Jesus to him (Acts 8:32).

The Eunuch was reading from the Isaiah 53:7-8, which is a prophecy about Jesus. Isaiah 53 has twenty-four prophetic points about the Messiah. Even Jesus claimed that Isaiah 53 was talking about Him (Mk. 10:45; Lk. 22:37). These Scriptures prophesied how Jesus would be led as an innocent sheep to the slaughter to be sacrificed for others. He did this voluntarily without murmuring or complaining. Even though He humbly submitted to His accusers and was proclaimed innocent by Pilate, the Jews insisted that He be put to death. Since Jesus' generation was responsible for putting Him on the cross, this is the reason it says: "And who will declare His generation? For His life is taken from the earth." In other words, who is going to describe this wicked generation who crucified the Messiah?

The eunuch wanted to know who this prophecy concerned. Was it about Isaiah or someone else? Philip took this opportunity to answer his question by preaching to him about Jesus from Isaiah 53. We are not told exactly what Philip taught him, but we can know that he taught him the same basic message he taught the Samaritans. He would have taught him about Jesus' death, burial, and resurrection and what he needed to do to be saved.

Now as they went down the road, they came to some water. And the eunuch said, "See, *here is* water. What hinders me from being baptized?" Then Philip said, "If you believe with all your heart, you may." And he answered and said, "I believe that Jesus Christ is the Son of God" (Acts 8:36-37).

These verses prove they were not in a dry desert because they had come near a pool of water. As Philip preached to him about Jesus and what was needed to be saved, he taught him about the necessity of baptism. We can know this because, when the eunuch saw the pool of water on the side of the road, he immediately wanted to know if there was anything preventing him from being baptized, which shows his eagerness to become a Christian.

Some Bible versions may or may not have verse 37 because it is not found in any of the earlier manuscripts, but it can be found in the later ones starting around the sixth century. However, part of the Ethiopian's confession of faith in Christ was quoted by Irenaeus in the second century (*Ante-Nicene Fathers Vol. 1 Against Heresies*, III.xii:8), which gives us some external evidence close to the first century that suggests that it belongs there. Whether this verse belongs or not does not take away from the question the eunuch asked. It is also interesting that the answer and response given in verse 37 fits naturally within in the text and agrees scripturally with the whole counsel of God.

Philip said that he must believe with all his heart, and the eunuch makes the confession that Jesus is the Son of God, which agrees with what Jesus said: "He who believes and is baptized will be saved; but he who does not believe will be condemned" (Mk. 16:16).

A person must believe before he can be baptized, which disproves the false doctrine of infant baptism because a baby cannot believe. These verses prove that the baptism Jesus was commanding and the baptism being taught by His disciples was water baptism. It also proves that a person's baptism is crucial to his salvation, and it should not be scheduled as some do in the religious world. The eunuch did not schedule his baptism at some later date so his family members could watch it. No, he saw the water on the side of the road, and he wanted to be baptized right away. Every time we see a conversion in the Bible, the person is always baptized immediately without delay.

So he commanded the chariot to stand still. And both Philip and the eunuch went down into the water, and he

66

baptized him. **Now when they came up out of the water, the Spirit of the Lord caught Philip away, so that the eunuch saw him no more; and he went on his way rejoicing. But Philip was found at Azotus. And passing through, he preached in all the cities till he came to Caesarea (Acts 8:38-40).**

The eunuch commanded the chariot to stop, and they went down into the water. Philip baptized him, and they came up out of the water. Those who teach that pouring or sprinkling is a valid way to baptize will say that they went to the edge of the water and Philip either took a cup and poured some water on him, or perhaps put his fingers in the water and sprinkled him. We can know this is not true because the Greek word that has been transliterated baptism means to dip, plunge, or immerse. Besides, the text says they went **into** the water and came **out of** the water, which proves they did not just go to the edge of the water. If pouring or sprinkling is acceptable, it would not make much sense for them to go into the water and get themselves all wet when they could have stood at the edge of the water.

When they came out of the water, the Holy Spirit sent Philip to a new area, and the eunuch continued his journey home rejoicing because he knew he was saved. Rejoicing was the typical response of those who had been baptized (Acts 16:34). The eunuch had a lot to rejoice about because he would no loner have to worship God from a distance outside the Jerusalem temple. Now he would be able to worship God in a local congregation with his brothers and sisters in Christ.

In conclusion, these two conversions have taught us that we must be taught about Jesus, which includes the simple plan of salvation. We must believe that Jesus is the Son of God, be willing to repent, be willing to confess that Jesus is the Son of God, and we must submit ourselves to baptism in water for the remission of our sins. Until we are baptized in the name of Jesus, we have nothing to rejoice about because without being baptized for the right reason we are hopelessly lost.

Questions

1. Discuss the origin of the Samaritans.
2. Why was Peter and John sent to Samaria?
3. Were the Samaritans saved before or after Peter and John came to them?
4. Was Philip in a dry desert when he met the eunuch?
5. How could Philip use Isaiah 53 to preach about Jesus?
6. Can a person be scripturally baptized if they do not believe?

THE CONVERSION OF SAUL
Acts 9, 22, 26   6

Out of all the conversions in the New Testament, Saul's is the most revealing and detailed. Not only does Saul's conversion prove that baptism is essential for salvation, it offers strong proof that Jesus was raised from the dead. Luke recounts Saul's conversion in Acts 9 from a historical perspective, while Acts 22 and 26 recounts it from Saul's perspective. Each account offers its own unique information of what happened during his conversion. So, we will examine Saul's conversion from all three accounts.

Then Saul, still breathing threats and murder against the disciples of the Lord, went to the high priest and asked letters from him to the synagogues of Damascus, so that if he found any who were of the Way, whether men or women, he might bring them bound to Jerusalem (Acts 9:1-2).

The first time Saul appears in the New Testament is on the occasion when Stephen was being stoned to death by the opposing Jews. These Jews laid their clothes at Saul's feet (Acts 7:58), and he approved of what they did to Stephen (Acts 8:1). This brutal murder was the beginning of the first great persecution of the church, and Saul was passionate about destroying anyone following Christ (Acts 8:3; 22:3-4; 26:9-11;

69

Gal. 1:13). Saul was not satisfied with persecuting the disciples of Jesus in Jerusalem alone. He wanted to go to Damascus, which was around 140 miles away, and seek them out there as well. It did not matter if it was a woman or a man, he wanted them all to be imprisoned or put to death.

Saul went to the high priest to get letters that would give him authorization to arrest any disciples of Christ he found in their synagogues at Damascus. Since there were multiple synagogues, this suggests there was a large Jewish population there. Josephus confirms this because he wrote that Nero slaughtered 18,000 Jews, including women and children (*Wars of the Jews* 2.20.2; 7.8.7).

Once Saul went to the high priest, who was the head of the Sanhedrin Council, he obtained the authority and commission of the chief priests (Acts 26:12). The chief priests all held the position of high priest at one time, and they still had a great influence on the decisions that were made. They were against Jesus' cause from the beginning, and they were still opposed to it.

As he journeyed he came near Damascus, and suddenly a light shone around him from heaven. Then he fell to the ground, and heard a voice saying to him, "Saul, Saul, why are you persecuting Me?" (Acts 9:3-4).

Saul was full of anticipation as he made his way to Damascus, which would turn out to be a life-changing event for him. His weeklong journey to Damascus was almost over, but around noon, suddenly without warning, a great light (Acts 22:6) brighter than the sun was shining around Saul and those who were traveling with him (Acts 26:13). This bright light caused all of them to fall to the ground (Acts 26:14). Some think Saul and his companions were riding horses, and they fell off their horses when this happened. However, horses are not mentioned in the text anywhere. Next, Saul hears a voice saying, "Saul, Saul, why are you persecuting Me?"

And he said, "Who are You, Lord?" Then the Lord said, "I am Jesus, whom you are persecuting. It *is* hard for you to kick against the goads" (Acts 9:5).

At this point, Saul did not know who was speaking to him, which is the reason he asked, "Who are You, Lord?" The term *Lord* was sometimes used in a similar way as we call someone *sir* today, while other times it was used to refer to Jesus. Since Saul did not know who He was, it is obvious that he was not calling Him Lord because He was Jesus. Some claim that Saul was saved when he hit the ground, but if this is correct, then he was saved before he knew Jesus.

Jesus answered his question in Hebrew saying, "I am Jesus, whom you are persecuting" (Acts 26:14). Grammatically He is saying, whom you are continuing to persecute. So, when someone persecutes the church, like Saul was doing, they are persecuting Jesus. The church is Jesus' body (Col. 1:18), which is made up of individual Christians (1 Cor. 12:27), and He is the head of that body (Col. 1:24). When we are baptized into that body (1 Cor. 12:13), God adds us to the church (Acts 2:47), which Jesus will save (Eph. 5:23). So, when we become members of that one body (Eph. 4:4), we are supposed to rejoice and mourn for one another (1 Cor. 12:26) just as Jesus rejoices and mourns for us as a good shepherd would (Jn. 10:11).

Jesus also told Saul, "It *is* hard for you to kick against the goads." According to Acts 26:14, Jesus said this before Saul asked who he was talking to, but Acts 9:5 shows Jesus saying it after his question. This chronological difference does not do any harm to the text because it does not matter if it was said before or after Saul's question. All that is important is that He said it. However, please note that most Bible versions do not have Jesus' statement in Acts 9:5 because there is a lack of textual evidence for it, but all the versions have it in Acts 26:14, which strongly suggests that Jesus made His statement before Saul's question.

To help us understand what Jesus is talking about, we need understand what a goad is: "A pointed stick used in driving draft animals - 'goad.' ...'to kick against the goad' (Acts 26.14), meaning to hurt oneself by active resistance" (Louw-Nida). A goad was used to motivate animals to move, and if they resisted, it caused them to endure more pain. These were used often on oxen that were being used to plow a field. According to the *Easton's Bible Dictionary*, this phrase *kick against the goads,* "...was proverbial for unavailing resistance to superior power."

Saul was kicking against the goads. He was an intelligent man who knew the Scriptures, and he had heard what was being taught about Jesus. The truth was there, but he had resisted it and now the truth was undeniable because Jesus appeared before him and spoke to him. Before we go any further in Acts 9, we need to examine what else Jesus said to Saul in Acts 26.

But rise and stand on your feet; for I have appeared to you for this purpose, to make you a minister and a witness both of the things which you have seen and of the things which I will yet reveal to you (Acts 26:16).

Jesus commanded Saul to rise to his feet, and He told him the reason He appeared to him. He wanted to make him a minister and a witness of the things he had just experienced and a witness of the things that would be revealed to him later (Acts 18:9; 22:17-21; 23:11; 27:23-24; 2 Cor. 12:2; Gal. 1:12). Since Saul was an eyewitness of Jesus, it made it possible for him to become one of the apostles (Acts 9:17; 1 Cor. 9:1; 15:8).

"I will deliver you from the *Jewish* people, as well as *from* the Gentiles, to whom I now send you, to open their eyes, *in order* to turn *them* from darkness to light, and *from* the power of Satan to God, that they may receive forgiveness of sins and an inheritance among those who are sanctified by faith in Me" (Acts 26:17-18).

When Jesus said He would deliver him from these people, He did not mean that Saul would not face persecution or difficult times (Acts 9:15-16; 2 Cor. 11:23-27). He simply meant that his life would be spared, and it was on many occasions (Acts 21-23, 27-28). The purpose of Saul's future ministry was to open people's eyes to the truth about Christ so they might turn away from the darkness of sin to the light of righteousness. If we are willing to obey God's Word, we can receive the forgiveness of our sins and an eternal home in heaven.

Notice how the forgiveness of sins is associated with being sanctified. We learn how to be sanctified by studying God's Word (Jn. 17:17) and by obeying it (1 Pet. 1:22-23). Paul teaches that sanctification is associated with baptism (1 Cor. 6:11), which makes sense because baptism is for the forgiveness of sins (Acts 2:38).

After this, Paul told King Agrippa: "I was not disobedient to the heavenly vision, but declared first to those in Damascus and in Jerusalem, and throughout all the region of Judea, and *then* to the Gentiles, that they should repent, turn to God, and do works befitting repentance" (Acts 26:19-20). While Paul only told part of the story here, he claimed that he did not disobey the heavenly vision, which teaches us that Saul had a choice to obey or disobey, but he chose to obey. God did not force him to become a Christian, just like He does not force anyone to become one.

Paul preached that a person "should repent, turn to God, and do works befitting repentance" (Acts 26:20). This proves that more than belief in Jesus and repentance is required to be saved because turning to God is something that happens after repentance. We learned in an earlier chapter that turning to the Lord refers to baptism (see my comments on Acts 2:38), which fits perfectly with verse 18 because it shows that those who turn to God receive the forgiveness of sins.

So he, trembling and astonished, said, "Lord, what do You want me to do?" Then the Lord *said* to him, "Arise and go into the city, and you will be told what you must do" (Acts 9:6).

The first part of this verse, including Saul's question, is not found in most Bible versions because of a lack of textual evidence. However, Saul's question is implied by Jesus' response, and we learn from Acts 22:10 that Saul did ask this question because that verse is found in all the Bible versions. Now that Saul had been humbled before Jesus and knew who He was, he wanted to know what he must do. Saul's response was similar to those Jews on the day of Pentecost who were pricked in their heart after they realized that Jesus was the Messiah (Acts 2:37). Since Saul wanted to know what he must do proves that he was not saved at this point. This time when Saul used the word *Lord*, he seemed to be recognizing Jesus as Lord and not just calling Him *sir* again.

Jesus wanted Saul to get up and go into the city where he would be told what he must do. Notice, there was something Saul would have to do to be saved. Why did Jesus not tell him what he needed to do to be saved? The answer is found in The Great Commission. Jesus put the teaching of salvation in the hands of humans (Mt. 28:19-20). For instance, an angel told Philip where to go to meet with the eunuch (Acts 8:26), and the Holy Spirit told him to overtake his chariot (Acts 8:29). It is the responsibility of Christians to teach others what they must do to be saved just as Philip taught the eunuch (Acts 8:30ff). This example is repeated in the conversion of Cornelius because an angel appeared to him and said: "Send men to Joppa, and call for Simon whose surname is Peter, 'who will tell you words by which you and all your household will be saved" (Acts 11:13-14). If it was God's plan for the words of salvation to be taught by those from heaven, this angel could have done it without involving Peter. These examples show that it is our responsibility to teach the plan of salvation. As we will see, Ananias is going to be the person that tells Saul what he must do to be saved.

And the men who journeyed with him stood speechless, hearing a voice but seeing no one (Acts 9:7).

These men did not have the same experience as Saul because they did not hear or see the same thing that Saul did. Notice what Saul said about this in Acts 22:9: "And those who were with me indeed saw the light and were afraid, but they did not hear the voice of Him who spoke to me." From this verse, we learn that they saw a light, but they did not see Jesus. In this account, Saul said they did not hear the voice, but in Acts 9 it states they heard a voice. Is this a contradiction? On the surface it might look like one, but it is not because the Greek word *phone* can be translated sound or voice. So, Acts 9:7 is saying that they heard a sound, but Acts 22:9 is saying they did not hear the actual voice or words of Jesus. A similar event happened when God spoke from heaven and some heard a noise, but they did not understand the words that were spoken (Jn. 12:28-29). There will always be those who try to find contradictions in God's Word, but when we examine the Scriptures closely, we will find that no contradictions exist.

Then Saul arose from the ground, and when his eyes were opened he saw no one. But they led him by the hand and brought *him* into Damascus. And he was three days without sight, and neither ate nor drank (Acts 9:8-9).

75

This encounter with the glory of that light (Acts 22:11) left Saul blind, and he had to be led by the hand of those with him to Damascus. It would be interesting to know what happened to Saul's companions after they helped him get to the city, but we are not given any additional information about them. Once Saul was in the city, he remained blind for three days and nights, and he did not eat or drink during that time. He was also praying to God during that time as well (Acts 9:11). Saul's reaction to seeing Jesus and hearing His voice had made him a believer in Christ, and it made him realize that he had been trying to destroy what God had established. This new revelation led him to sorrow in a Godly manner (2 Cor. 7:9-10), and he was repenting for what he had done.

Many of those in the religious world would say that Saul was saved on the road to Damascus or that he was saved as he repented and prayed to God. If this is true, then Saul was the most miserable saved person in the Bible because the usual reaction to being saved was one of rejoicing (Acts 8:39; 16:34).

Now there was a certain disciple at Damascus named Ananias; and to him the Lord said in a vision, "Ananias." And he said, "Here I am, Lord." So the Lord *said* to him, "Arise and go to the street called Straight, and inquire at the house of Judas for *one* called Saul of Tarsus, for behold, he is praying. And in a vision he has seen a man named Ananias coming in and putting *his* hand on him, so that he might receive his sight." Then Ananias answered, "Lord, I have heard from many about this man, how much harm he has done to Your saints in Jerusalem. And here he has authority from the chief priests to bind all who call on Your name." But the Lord said to him, "Go, for he is a chosen vessel of Mine to bear My name before Gentiles, kings, and the children of Israel. For I will show him how many

things he must suffer for My name's sake" (Acts 9:10-16).

Ananias was a devout man who was well respected by his fellow Jews in Damascus (Acts 22:12). He was usually ready to serve God, but when Jesus asked him to go find Saul so that he might receive his sight and be told what he must do to be saved, he was a little hesitant. He wanted to make sure Jesus was sending him to the right man because the saints had told him stories about how Saul was persecuting the church. The term *saints* is just another name for Christians because all Christians are saints, which is in stark contrast with what the Catholic Church teaches about sainthood.

Ananias was supposed to go to the street called Straight and find the house of Judas. "It is believed this street is still in existence, but now it is called Derb el-Mustakim" (ISBE). We do not know anything about this Judas other than Saul was staying at his house. Jesus reassured Ananias that Saul is the right man for him to go to because Saul was chosen by God to be a vessel for Him. Saul being chosen by God does not mean he did not have a choice in the matter because he had a free will. Since God is omniscient, He could know beforehand that Saul would choose to be this vessel (Gal. 1:15-16).

Since Saul would be proclaiming the good news to Gentiles, kings, and the children of Israel, I believe he was fulfilling Isaiah's prophecy: "The Gentiles shall see your righteousness, And all kings your glory. You shall be called by a new name, Which the mouth of the LORD will name" (Isa. 62:2). The new name was Christian, and it was first used when Saul and Barnabas were at Antioch (Acts 11:26). As we learned earlier, Saul would have to endure many hardships as a Christian.

And Ananias went his way and entered the house; and laying his hands on him he said, "Brother Saul, the Lord Jesus, who appeared to you on the road as you came,

has sent me that you may receive your sight and be filled with the Holy Spirit." Immediately there fell from his eyes *something* like scales, and he received his sight at once; and he arose and was baptized (Acts 9:17-18).

Now that Ananias has been reassured by Jesus, he made his way to Saul. When he found him, he laid his hands on him and called him brother Saul. Since he called him brother, some claim that he was calling him a brother in Christ, proving that he was saved at this point. However, this is not true because it was a common practice for Jews to call each other brother, and we have examples of Christian Jews who called non-Christian Jews brother (Acts 2:29; 3:17; Rom. 9:3). So, calling him brother does not mean he was a Christian.

We also learn that Ananias was supposed to lay his hands on Saul so he could receive his sight (Acts 22:13). When he did, Saul received his sight that very hour, and he was able to look up at Ananias (Acts 22:13). We learned in the chapter, "Conversions by Philip the evangelist" that only the apostles could impart spiritual gifts, which means at some point Ananias had been given his ability to heal Saul's blindness by one of the apostles. Not only did he open his eyes so he could see, he also opened his eyes spiritually by telling him what he must do. Acts 9:17 teaches that Ananias would make it possible for Saul to receive his sight and be filled with the Holy Spirit. Since Ananias was not an apostle and could not impart spiritual gifts, we can know that being filled with the Holy Spirit does not refer to the miraculous gifts that came through the hands of an apostle.

Also, there is nothing in the text demanding that Saul receiving his sight and being filled with the Holy Spirit was going to happen at the same time. Instead, the most probable meaning of being filled with the Holy Spirit was the same promise that every Christian is given when they are baptized (Acts 2:38-39). This explanation fits perfectly with the text because verse

78

18 only says that Saul's eyes were healed when Ananias put his hands on him, and then he arose and was baptized. So, Ananias made it possible for him to receive the Holy Spirit by telling him what he must do.

Then he said, 'The God of our fathers has chosen you that you should know His will, and see the Just One, and hear the voice of His mouth. For you will be His witness to all men of what you have seen and heard' (Acts 22:14-15).

Saul had already seen the Lord and heard His voice. Now it was time for him to find out what he must do to be saved so he could begin his work as a witness of the things he had seen and heard.

At this point, Saul has believed in Jesus, confessed Him as Lord, repented, and prayed. However, we can know without a doubt that Saul was not saved on the road to Damascus or at this point because of what Ananias tells Saul:

And now why are you waiting? Arise and be baptized, and wash away your sins, calling on the name of the Lord (Acts 22:16).

If a person says that Saul was saved before this point, then he is going to have to say that he was saved while still stained with sin, which proves "the sinner's prayer" that many denominations proclaim as being the point of salvation is false. If anyone could have been saved by praying to God, it would have been Saul. However, we just learned from verse 16 that Saul was still lost in his sins, even though he had been praying to God. Besides, there is not one example of anyone being taught to say "the sinner's prayer" in the Bible. The origin of "the sinner's prayer" is not clear, but some believe it had its start in the early days of the Protestant Reformation movement, and it was made popular by men like Billy Graham.

Ananias understood the urgency of this situation because he wanted to know why Saul was waiting. He commanded him to arise and literally get himself baptized to wash away his sins.

> In Acts 22:16 it is used in the Middle Voice, in the command given to Saul of Tarsus, "arise and be baptized" the significance of the Middle Voice form being "get thyself baptized" (Vine).

Remember, Jesus said Saul would be told what he must do, which means there would be something he could do, and that was obeying the urgent command to arise and be baptized to wash away his sins. The fact that he had to arise teaches us two things about his baptism.

First, if baptism was done by sprinkling or pouring, he would not have to arise because he could have had someone sprinkle or pour some water on him.

Second, he was not talking about Holy Spirit baptism, since he would not have to arise for that either because it would not matter if he was lying down or standing on his head - he could be baptized by the Holy Spirit. The only baptism that fits this text is water baptism by immersion in the name of Jesus for the remission of sins. Even those who deny that baptism is for the remission of sins admit the language here and in other verses could mean that baptism is for the remission of sin. For instances notice what A.T. Robertson said:

> It is possible, as in 2:38, to take these words as teaching baptismal remission or salvation by means of baptism, but to do so is in my opinion a complete subversion of Saul's vivid and picturesque language. As in Rom. 6:4-6 where baptism is the picture of death, burial

and resurrection, so here baptism pictures the change that had already taken place when Saul surrendered to Jesus on the way (verse 10). Baptism here pictures the washing away of sins by the blood of Christ (Robertson).

He recognized the text grammatically says that baptism washes away a person's sins, but he denies it because of his personal opinion. Also, he wants to turn baptism into something a person does to show he already has the forgiveness of sin, but nothing in the text implies this idea. Besides, the Scriptures clearly show that Saul was **not** forgiven of his sins until he submitted to baptism.

Those who oppose the necessity of baptism also claim that *calling on the name of the Lord* is what washes away a person's sins and not baptism. They believe that *calling on the name of the Lord* is done by a person asking Jesus to come into his heart, but this is not true as we will see. I will admit that it is grammatically possible for *calling on the name of the Lord* to precede both *baptism* and *wash away your sins*. However, it also grammatically possible that *calling on the name of the Lord* occurs at the same time as *baptism* and *wash away your sins*. So, which is the correct one? To find our answer, we must examine the whole counsel of God, but first, notice what Wayne Jackson says:

> In submitting to immersion, one is actually by that act "calling on" the Lord's name. Lenski observes that the aorist participle, "calling on his name," is "either simultaneous with that of the aorist imperatives [get yourself immersed and washed] or immediately precedes it, the difference being merely formal" (1934, 909) (*The Acts of the Apostles* 286).

81

So, *be baptized* and *wash away your sins* are both aorist imperatives. Whenever the aorist tense is used together with the imperative mood, it indicates a great urgency for this command to be carried out. So the emphasis is on being baptized. As Wayne Jackson pointed out, *calling on the name of the Lord* is an aorist participle, and it is closely associated with the aorist imperatives *be baptized* and *wash away your sins*. So, it is grammatically possible that submitting yourself to baptism is to call on the name of the Lord.

Now, let's dig a little deeper and find out what else God's Word says about *calling on the name of the Lord*. On the day of Pentecost, Peter quotes Joel and said: "And it shall come to pass *That* whoever calls on the name of the LORD Shall be saved" (Acts 2:21). First, when the people heard this saying, they did not get the idea that all they had to do was ask Jesus into their heart. Instead, they asked Peter what they must do (Acts 2:37). Peter let them know that *calling on the name of the Lord* included repentance and baptism (Acts 2:38). Once again, this shows *calling on the name of the Lord* is associated with being baptized, and it is more than just invoking His name or asking Him into the heart to be saved. Jesus made it clear that it takes more than a verbal plea such as, "Lord, Lord," to be saved because a person must obey the Father's will (Mt. 7:21; Lk. 6:46). So, *calling on the name of the Lord* includes obeying the gospel (Rom.10:13 -16). Since *calling on the name of the Lord*, which includes baptism, is necessary to be saved, it proves that Saul was not saved at this point in his conversion because Ananias told him to call on the name of the Lord. Of course there are other verses that teach that baptism is necessary to be saved as well (Mk.16:16; 1 Pet.3:21).

Finally, notice what Paul tells the Corinthians:

And such were some of you. But you were washed, but you were sanctified, but you were justified in the name

of the Lord Jesus and by the Spirit of our God (1 Cor. 6:11).

Paul used the same word *washed* as Ananias did in Acts 22:16. He had just finished naming many sins that would keep a person from going to heaven. Then he lets the Corinthians know that they used to be guilty of those sins, but they had been washed, sanctified, and justified. In other words, their sins had been washed away, just like Saul's would be washed away when he submitted himself to baptism.

The word *wash* means to "wash off or away" (Thayer). When we think about washing off, we think about water and soap. Understanding this simple word should make us think about the water that we are baptized in and how Jesus' blood is the cleansing soap that removes the stain of sin from our souls (Rev. 1:5). There is nothing magical about the water; it is simply the place that God has designated where we will come in contact with the cleansing power of Jesus' blood. We know this is true by our faith in the working of God (Col. 2:12). It is difficult to understand how anyone could associate a verbal plea, or saying "the sinner's prayer" with the word *wash*. Both 1 Corinthians 6:11 and Acts 22:16 are talking about the same thing, which means our sins are washed away when we are baptized in water in the name of Jesus for the remission of our sins.

It is also interesting that this washing was done "in the name of the Lord Jesus and by the Spirit of our God" because it fits perfectly with The Great Commission (Mt. 28:19) and with what Peter taught on the day of Pentecost (Acts 2:38). We can see this idea of washing in several other passages as well (Heb. 10:22; Eph. 5:26; Titus 3:5). Notice what Thayer says about our two verses:

> … 1 Cor. 6:11 … Acts 22:16. For the sinner is unclean, polluted as it were by the filth of his

sins. Whoever obtains remission of sins has his sins put, so to speak, out of God's sight is cleansed from them in the sight of God. Remission is (represented as) obtained by undergoing baptism; hence, those who have gone down into the baptismal bath (lavacrum, cf. Titus 3:5; Eph. 5:26) are said to have washed themselves, or to have washed away their sins, i. e. to have been cleansed from their sins.

There should be no doubt for those who examine Saul's conversion with an honest heart that baptism is essential for salvation and it is the point at which a person's sins are washed away.

Not only does Saul's conversion teach us what is necessary to be saved, it offers strong proof that Jesus was raised from the dead. If I can prove that Jesus appeared to Saul on the road to Damascus, then I can prove that Jesus was raised from the dead. First, consider the following points about Saul's character before he went to Damascus:

- He was a fanatic, he persecuted the church beyond measure, and he advanced in the Jewish religion beyond those of his own age (Gal. 1:13-14).
- He consented to Stephen's death (Acts 7:58 –8:1).
- He drug both men and women to prison (Acts 8:1-3).
- He even went outside Jerusalem to take down Christianity (Acts 9:1-2).
- He said he was a Hebrew of the Hebrews and a Pharisee (Phi. 3:5).
- He told King Agrippa that he was exceedingly enraged against Christians (Acts 26:9-11).

Saul was at the top of his game. He was a local hero among his people, and he had power, wealth, and fame. The question becomes, "Who could have possibly changed Saul's mind about Christianity?" Could it have been some of his fellow men? No, they admired him. Could it have been another Christian? No, he would not have listened to them because he wanted them all dead or locked up. Maybe there was an ulterior motive for Saul to convert to Christianity. What could it have been? It was not wealth because we know he had to work with his own hands and went hungry at times (Acts 20: 33-34, 1 Cor. 4:11-12.) It was not for a better reputation or more power because he already had all that as a Pharisee. There is only one logical conclusion: only Jesus could have changed a man like this, just as the Bible records for us (Acts 9, 22, 26), which is why Saul's conversion offers strong proof that Jesus was raised from the dead.

In conclusion, we have learned many wonderful things from the conversion of Saul, including what it takes to be saved. We have seen strong proof that Jesus was raised from the dead. Now that you know what is required for the forgiveness of your sins, why are you waiting?

Questions

1. What did Jesus mean when He told Saul, "It is hard for you to kick against the goads?"
2. Explain the difference between what Saul and his companions heard and saw.
3. Did Ananias have the same ability as the apostles to impart miraculous gifts?
4. Discuss why Paul was not saved before he was baptized.
5. What do we learn from Saul being told to arise and be baptized?
6. How do we call on the name of the Lord?
7. What is the significance of the word *wash*?
8. How does Saul's conversion offer proof that Jesus was raised from the dead?

THE CONVERSION OF CORNELIUS
Acts 10 - 11

7

The conversion of Cornelius is one of the most misunderstood conversions in the Bible. Those who teach that water baptism is a sign that a person has already been saved believe this conversion proves their argument. However, as we examine Cornelius's conversion, we will discover that his conversion will agree with all the other conversions in the book of Acts, which teach that water baptism is necessary for salvation.

Acts 10 teaches us what happened at the conversion of Cornelius, but Acts 11 records the chronological order of the events that happened. Cornelius's conversion is similar to the conversion of the eunuch in that an angel and the Holy Spirit were involved in arranging a meeting between the lost and the preacher. Some estimate that around eight years have past since the day of Pentecost, and the gospel had not been preached to the Gentiles yet.

There was a certain man in Caesarea called Cornelius, a centurion of what was called the Italian Regiment, a devout _man_ and one who feared God with all his household, who gave alms generously to the people, and prayed to God always. About the ninth hour of the day he saw clearly in a vision an angel of God coming in and

saying to him, "Cornelius!" And when he observed him, he was afraid, and said, "What is it, lord?" So he said to him, "Your prayers and your alms have come up for a memorial before God. Now send men to Joppa, and send for Simon whose surname is Peter. He is lodging with Simon, a tanner, whose house is by the sea. He will tell you what you must do." And when the angel who spoke to him had departed, Cornelius called two of his household servants and a devout soldier from among those who waited on him continually. So when he had explained all *these* things to them, he sent them to Joppa (Acts 10:1-8).

Caesarea was an important seaport. It was a city built by Herod the Great between 25 and 13 B.C., and it was named in honor of Caesar Augustus (Nelson's New Illustrated Bible Dictionary 235). Cornelius was a centurion of the Italian Regiment. The regiment consisted of about 600 men, and each Centurion was over 100 men. Cornelius was a devout man, which meant he was pious or reverent toward God. He and his household, including his slaves, feared God, which means he respected God, and he did not worship idols associated with paganism. We can also know that he was not a proselyte because he had not been circumcised (Acts 11:3). Those who became proselytes would become like Jews by being circumcised; then they would be baptized, and an animal would be sacrificed for them. Even though Cornelius was not a proselyte, he was seeking after God, gave alms to the people, and he prayed to God always. He had a good reputation among the Jews (Acts 10:22), which implies that he gave part of his alms to the Jews, and he followed their tradition of prayer. The Jews prayed three times a day: 9 A.M., 12 P.M., and 3 P.M.

At 3 P.M., Cornelius had a vision of angel in his home. The angel spoke his name, and as he observed the angel it made him afraid. Even though this man was in charge of 100 men, this encounter humbled him and caused him to be afraid. Cornelius had never seen such a sight, and I suspect that anyone who saw this would experience a similar fear. Cornelius wanted to know the reason this angel was appearing before him so he asked, "What is it, Lord?"

The angel replied: "Your prayers and your alms have come up for a memorial before God. Now send men to Joppa, and send for Simon whose surname is Peter. He is lodging with Simon, a tanner, whose house is by the sea. He will tell you what you must do." We learn from Acts 11:14 that the angel also said that Peter "will tell you words by which you and your household will be saved." Even though Cornelius was a just man who feared God, this angel made it clear that he was lost because he had to hear the words of Peter to be saved. This example proves that a person can be a kind moral person who respects God yet can still be lost if he has not heard and obeyed the Word of God. This example also shows that salvation does not come from praying to God.

Some people might see a contradiction here because the blind man that Jesus healed said: "Now we know that God does not hear sinners; but if anyone is a worshiper of God and does His will, He hears him" (Jn. 9:31). Even though this is recording the words of an uninspired man, this idea is taught throughout the Old Testament (Ps. 34:15; Prov. 1:28-31, 15:29, 28:9; Mic. 3:4; Zech. 7:12-13). When we examine these verses, we will find that God does not hear the prayer of those who are not willing to hear or obey the Law of God. However, if a person is seeking after God, and he is trying to obey God's Word, God will hear his prayer, just like he heard Cornelius's prayer. Even the blind man in John 9 said: "If anyone is a worshiper of God and does His will, He hears him" (Jn. 9:31). Many other passages imply this truth as well (Prov. 8:17; Acts 10:4; Jas. 4:8).

In the conversion of the eunuch, the angel told Philip where to go, but in Cornelius's conversion, the angel is telling the sinner whom to send for so he can hear the words that will save him. If it was God's plan for angels to preach the gospel to the sinner, this angel could have done it. However, as we have already learned from the previous conversions, this responsibility was given to humans. After hearing the instructions from the angel, Cornelius sent two of his servants and one of his soldiers to Joppa to bring back Peter.

Joppa was a seaport city located about 30 miles northwest of Jerusalem and 30 miles south of Caesarea. Peter was staying with a tanner. A tanner worked with animal skins making them into leather and other useful items. They usually lived close to the sea for two reasons:

> a) There was a terrible smell associated with their work; the sea breezes would help to diffuse the noxious fumes, and b) Sea water was used in processing the hides (Jackson, *The Acts of the Apostles* 123).

The next day, as they went on their journey and drew near the city, Peter went up on the housetop to pray, about the sixth hour. Then he became very hungry and wanted to eat; but while they made ready, he fell into a trance and saw heaven opened and an object like a great sheet bound at the four corners, descending to him and let down to the earth. In it were all kinds of four-footed animals of the earth, wild beasts, creeping things, and birds of the air. And a voice came to him, "Rise, Peter; kill and eat." But Peter said, "Not so, Lord! For I have never eaten anything common or unclean." And a voice *spoke* to him again the second time, "What God has cleansed you must not call common." This was done three times. And the object was taken up into heaven again (Acts 10:9-16).

Peter was waiting for the meal to be cooked, and he went up on the roof to pray around noon. The typical house back then had a flat roof with stairs leading up to it from the outside. Not only was it common for people to go up on the roof to pray, they also used their roofs in the following ways:

- Preaching (Mt. 10:27).
- Drying out crops (Jos. 2:6).
- Sleeping in the summer to stay cool.
- Entertaining guests. (Since this was a common practice, a law was made to build a rail around the roof to prevent people from falling off [Deut. 22:8]).
- Having religious discussions.
- Lodging strangers.
- During the feast of the Tabernacles they would set up tents on their roofs to live in (Ex. 23:16).

Peter was extremely hungry when he fell into a trance. Then he saw heaven open, and down came an object that was like a great sheet. On this sheet was a mixture of clean and unclean animals. Unclean animals were prohibited for the Jew to eat under the Law of Moses (Lev. 11; Deut. 14). The heavenly voice said, "Rise, Peter; kill and eat." In Peter's entire life, he had never eaten anything that was unclean, and he was not about to start now, which is why he refused to do it.

This time the heavenly voice said, "What God has cleansed you must not call common." This was done three times before Peter came out of his trance. Since Peter would not eat the unclean food, obviously he did not know yet that all food was made clean under the new covenant (1 Tim. 4:3-4; Mk. 7:19). In fact, no Christian is obligated to keep the Law of Moses because that obligation was taken away at the cross and made obsolete (Col. 2:14; Eph. 2:14-15; Heb. 8:13). We are only obligated to keep the commands found in the Law of

Christ under the new covenant (Heb. 7:19, 22; 8:6-8, 13; 9:15; 1 Cor. 9:21).

We need to realize that the apostles received their miraculous knowledge in part (1 Cor. 13:9). Even when they spoke by the inspiration of the Holy Spirit, sometimes they did not fully understand what they were saying until later, which proves that they were speaking by the inspiration of the Holy Spirit. A great example of this can be found on the day of Pentecost when Peter said: "Repent, and let every one of you be baptized in the name of Jesus Christ for the remission of sins; and you shall receive the gift of the Holy Spirit. For the promise is to you and to your children, and to all who are afar off, as many as the Lord our God will call" (Acts 2:38-39). Notice, the promise of salvation was for both Jews and Gentiles because those *who are afar off* are Gentiles (Eph. 2:13, 17). However, we learn that neither Peter nor any other Christian had taught the gospel to the Gentiles up to this point, which proves that Peter did not fully understand what he said on Pentecost, but he is about to. Just as these unclean foods were no longer unclean under the new covenant, the Gentiles are no longer unclean or unacceptable to hear the good of news of Jesus. Peter's vision taught him this.

Now while Peter wondered within himself what this vision which he had seen meant, behold, the men who had been sent from Cornelius had made inquiry for Simon's house, and stood before the gate. And they called and asked whether Simon, whose surname was Peter, was lodging there. While Peter thought about the vision, the Spirit said to him, "Behold, three men are seeking you."Arise therefore, go down and go with them, doubting nothing; for I have sent them." Then Peter went down to the men who had been sent to him from Cornelius, and said, "Yes, I am he whom you seek. For what reason have you come?" And they said, "Cornelius *the* centurion, a just man, one who fears God

and has a good reputation among all the nation of the Jews, was divinely instructed by a holy angel to summon you to his house, and to hear words from you." Then he invited them in and lodged *them* (Acts 10:17-23).

Peter was perplexed at what he saw, and he was trying to figure it out as these men from Cornelius's household began asking for him at Simon's gate. While Peter continued to go over this vision in his head, the Holy Spirit told him: "Behold, three men are seeking you. Arise therefore, go down and go with them, doubting nothing; for I have sent them." The Holy Spirit's message teaches us that He was the one that sent the angel to Cornelius. Now He is telling Peter to go with these three men without doubting. Peter obeys the Holy Spirit, and he goes down and talks with these three men.

Peter wanted to know what these men wanted, and they began to tell him about Cornelius and how he was divinely instructed to send for him. Apparently Peter was beginning to understand his vision because he invited these Gentiles into Simon's house to stay the night, which was unheard of for a Jew.

On the next day Peter went away with them, and some brethren from Joppa accompanied him. And the following day they entered Caesarea. Now Cornelius was waiting for them, and had called together his relatives and close friends. As Peter was coming in, Cornelius met him and fell down at his feet and worshiped *him*. But Peter lifted him up, saying, "Stand up; I myself am also a man." And as he talked with him, he went in and found many who had come together. Then he said to them, "You know how unlawful it is for a Jewish man to keep company with or go to one of another nation. But God has shown me that I should not call any man common or unclean. "Therefore I came without

93

objection as soon as I was sent for. I ask, then, for what reason have you sent for me? (Acts 10:23-29).

On the third day, Peter went with these Gentiles, and he took along six Jewish brethren (Acts 11:12). Since Jews learned from an early age not to associate with Gentiles, it must have been hard for them overcome their prejudice and go with Peter, which shows how these men were willing to overlook their traditions and allow God to be their guide. They broke their thirty mile trip into two days, and they arrived at Cornelius's house on the fourth day. Cornelius was excited about seeing Peter, and he gathered his relatives and close friends because he wanted them to hear the words that would save them. This shows that Cornelius was not just concerned about his own soul. If you have ever waited on someone to arrive at your house that you really wanted to see, then you have a general idea of how Cornelius felt as he patiently waited for Peter.

When Peter entered Cornelius's house, Cornelius fell down before him and worshipped him. However, Peter would not allow him to continue to do this. Instead, he told him to stand up because he is only a man. Peter knew that only God deserved worship like that (Rev. 22:8-9). When we compare Peter's humbleness to the pope of the Catholic Church, there is a big difference because the pope never keeps people from bowing down and worshipping him.

Peter saw that many had come together at Cornelius's house, and he told them it was unlawful for a Jew to keep company with a foreigner. There is nothing specifically stated in the Old Testament that teaches this that I am aware of. However, this had become part of the Jewish tradition (Acts 11:2-3; 22:21-22; Jn. 4:27; 18:28). Even though this teaching was part of Peter's life, he overlooked it because God was telling him not to call any human common or unclean. Again, Peter wants to know what Cornelius wants from him.

94

So Cornelius said, "Four days ago I was fasting until this hour; and at the ninth hour I prayed in my house, and behold, a man stood before me in bright clothing, and said, 'Cornelius, your prayer has been heard, and your alms are remembered in the sight of God. Send therefore to Joppa and call Simon here, whose surname is Peter. He is lodging in the house of Simon, a tanner, by the sea. When he comes, he will speak to you.' So I sent to you immediately, and you have done well to come. Now therefore, we are all present before God, to hear all the things commanded you by God" (Acts 10:30-33).

Cornelius told Peter about the events that happened four days ago at 3 P.M. This time, he described the appearance of the angel as being in bright clothing. As we discussed earlier, Cornelius's prayer was heard, but he was still lost because he still had to hear the words that would save him (Acts 11:14). Now Cornelius and those with him were ready to hear the message and learn what they must do to save their souls.

Then Peter opened *his* mouth and said: "In truth I perceive that God shows no partiality. But in every nation whoever fears Him and works righteousness is accepted by Him. The word which *God* sent to the children of Israel, preaching peace through Jesus Christ -- He is Lord of all -- that word you know, which was proclaimed throughout all Judea, and began from Galilee after the baptism which John preached: how God anointed Jesus of Nazareth with the Holy Spirit and with power, who went about doing good and healing all who were oppressed by the devil, for God was with Him" (Acts 10:34-38).

Peter began to preach to them. It was a hard lesson for Peter to learn, but he realized that God does not show partiality between Jews and Gentiles. Those who fear Him and work righteousness will be accepted by Him. Those who teach there are no works involved in our salvation have missed the mark because Peter has taught us that we must fear God and do works of righteousness. Works of righteousness are works of obedience and not works of merit (Phil. 2:12; Acts 26:20; Heb. 5:8-9).

Now Peter knows that the gospel is for both Jews and Gentiles because "He is Lord of all." Peter teaches us that Cornelius had some knowledge of Jesus since His ministry had been proclaimed throughout Judea. When we consider all the miracles and signs Jesus did, including the people He healed and the demons he cast out, we can understand why all of Palestine would have heard something about Him including Cornelius.

"And we are witnesses of all things which He did both in the land of the Jews and in Jerusalem, whom they killed by hanging on a tree. Him God raised up on the third day, and showed Him openly, not to all the people, but to witnesses chosen before by God, *even* to us who ate and drank with Him after He arose from the dead. And He commanded us to preach to the people, and to testify that it is He who was ordained by God *to be* Judge of the living and the dead. To Him all the prophets witness that, through His name, whoever believes in Him will receive remission of sins" (Acts 10:39-43).

Peter confirmed that Jesus is the Son of God and that he and the other apostles were eyewitnesses of all the things that Jesus did during His ministry. He pointed out that Jesus was hung on a tree, which refers to His crucifixion, and how God raised Him up on the third day. Jesus was seen alive by over 500 witnesses after His death (1 Cor. 15:6). Next, Peter taught them how Jesus will be the judge of the living and the dead, and how all the prophets from the Old Testament "witness that, through His name, whoever believes in Him will receive remission of sins." When we examine the Old Testament prophets, we can see how all them talked about the coming Messiah and what He would do, which is why Paul said: "Therefore the law was our tutor *to bring us* to Christ, that we might be justified by faith" (Gal. 3:24), and "For whatever things were written before were written for our learning, that we through the patience and comfort of the Scriptures might have hope" (Rom. 15:4, see also Acts 3:24).

Some will take verse 43 and try to make it teach the "faith only" doctrine. If we are willing to say this verse is teaching that belief alone saves a person, then we must exclude grace, repentance, confession, and baptism. The word *believes* is used as a synecdoche, which means a part that stands for the whole. So, *believes* represents an obedient faith, which includes everything that is necessary for salvation.

While Peter was still speaking these words, the Holy Spirit fell upon all those who heard the word. And those of the circumcision who believed were astonished, as many as came with Peter, because the gift of the Holy Spirit had been poured out on the Gentiles also. For they heard them speak with tongues and magnify God. Then Peter answered, "Can anyone forbid water, that these should not be baptized who have received the Holy Spirit just as we *have?"* And he commanded them to be baptized in the name of the Lord. Then they asked him to stay a few days (Acts 10:44-48).

We find out that Peter was still preaching these words when the Holy Spirit fell upon them. Since this happened, some have determined that Cornelius's household was saved at that moment, which would mean that a person is saved before he is water baptized. However, this is not true. First, no one can produce a verse in the Bible that states that Holy Spirit baptism saves a person. Second, Holy Spirit baptism is only recorded two times in Scripture, once here and at the day of Pentecost (Acts 2). Third, we need to remember that these men had to hear the words that Peter had to say so they could be saved (Acts 10:6; 11:14).

However, we learn that Peter was not finished preaching to them about Jesus (Acts 10:44). When we look at Acts 11, which is a chronological account of these events (Acts 11:4), we discover that Peter had just began speaking when it was interrupted by this event (Acts 11:15). The word *began* comes from the Greek word *archo*, which: "Indicates that a thing was but just begun when it was interrupted by something else ... Acts 11:15" (Thayer).

This means that Peter had just barely begun speaking when the Holy Spirit fell on them. If Holy Spirit baptism saved them, it did so before they heard the words they needed to hear to be saved. At the Jerusalem meeting in Acts 15, Peter mentioned this event and said: "So God, who knows the heart, acknowledged them by giving them the Holy Spirit, just as *He did* to us, and made no distinction between us and them, purifying their hearts by faith" (Acts 15:8-9). If Holy Spirit baptism saved them, then we have a problem because Peter said their hearts were purified by faith, which includes obeying the Word of God (1 Pet. 1:22). How could they have this kind of faith when they had just barely heard a small part of Peter's lesson? The Bible makes it clear that without faith it is impossible to please God (Heb. 11:6), which proves that they were not saved by Holy Spirit baptism.

So, why was the Holy Spirit poured out at this time? It was done to prove to Peter and all those present that God accepted the Gentiles as being His people, and they needed to hear the gospel. To prove this further, notice what Peter said in his defense to the Jews in Jerusalem who did not like what Peter did (Acts 11:2-3).

"And as I began to speak, the Holy Spirit fell upon them, as upon us at the beginning. Then I remembered the word of the Lord, how He said, 'John indeed baptized with water, but you shall be baptized with the Holy Spirit.' If therefore God gave them the same gift as *He gave* us when we believed on the Lord Jesus Christ, who was I that I could withstand God?" When they heard these things they became silent; and they glorified God, saying, "Then God has also granted to the Gentiles repentance to life." (Acts 11:15-18)

When this event happened, Peter remembered the words of John the Baptist and how Jesus would baptize with the Holy Spirit. Since Jesus would administer Holy Spirit baptism, which was a promise, it proves that the baptism He commanded His disciples in The Great Commission was not Holy Spirit baptism. Joel prophesied that the Spirit would be poured out on all flesh (Joel 2:28ff), which would include both Jews and Gentiles. It was poured out on the apostles on the day of Pentecost (Acts 2:1-4, 16ff,) and now it had been poured out on the Gentiles, which fulfilled Joel's prophecy.

We can see that Holy Spirit baptism was not a common occurrence because Peter had to remember all the way back to the day of Pentecost for an example of Holy Spirit baptism. If Holy Spirit baptism is what saves, then Peter could have recalled any conversion to compare it to instead of having to go all the way back to the day of Pentecost. This fact proves that Holy Spirit baptism was not a common occurrence. Once these Jews heard the truth on this matter it was settled. If God was willing to give the Gentiles the Holy Spirit directly from heaven like He did for the apostles on the day of Pentecost, then no one was going stand in the way of God's truth. This is the reason they rejoiced that God had given the Gentiles access to repentance of life.

When the Holy Spirit fell upon Cornelius's household, they all began to speak in different languages just like the apostles did on the day of Pentecost, which made Peter and his companions amazed. Now that Peter knows without a doubt that the Gentiles have been accepted by God, he finished speaking the words they needed to hear to be saved. Peter asked: "Can anyone forbid water, that these should not be baptized who have received the Holy Spirit just as we *have*?" (Acts 10:47). After they witnessed God's approval for the Gentiles, no one would object to these Gentiles being saved. So Peter "commanded them to be baptized in the name of the Lord" (Acts 10:48).

Just as Peter commanded the Jews on the day of Pentecost: "Repent, and let every one of you be baptized in the name of Jesus Christ for the remission of sins" (Acts 2:38), he commanded the Gentiles to do the same. We can know that he is talking about water baptism because he asked if anyone could forbid water. Since this was a command that could be followed, it confirms that the one baptism that saves (Eph. 4:5) is water baptism.

One last point needs to be made from Acts 11.

Now the apostles and brethren who were in Judea heard that the Gentiles had also received the word of God (Acts 1:11).

This verse means that the Gentiles heard the same basic message the Jews heard on the day of Pentecost, and notice what happened to those that received that message:

Then those who gladly received his word were baptized; and that day about three thousand souls were added *to them* (Acts 2:41).

When they heard the words they needed to hear to be saved, they received them and they were baptized, which proves that receiving God's Word includes baptism for both Jews and Gentiles.

Even though Cornelius's conversion is often misunderstood, it is easy to understand that it does not contradict the other conversions in the book of Acts. Instead, it agrees with them and the other Scriptures that teach what we must do to be saved. Those who are looking for a way to divorce water baptism from the plan of salvation will not find what they are looking for in this conversion or anywhere else in the New Testament.

Questions

1. Discuss Cornelius's background and devotion to God.
2. Was Cornelius's prayers heard?
3. Name some of the ways people used their flat roofs.
4. Why did Peter tell Cornelius to stand up when he tried to worship him?
5. Does Acts 10:43 prove that we are saved by faith alone?
6. Did Holy Spirit baptism save Cornelius and those in his house? Why or why not?
7. Why did Cornelius and those in his house receive Holy Spirit baptism?

Paul was one of the hardest working apostles (1 Cor. 15:10), and he established many churches. He was responsible for many conversions, but only a few of them are mentioned in the Bible. We will examine three of these conversions beginning with the conversion of Lydia and her household.

In Acts 16, Silas joined Paul on his second missionary journey, and they traveled to Derbe and Lystra. While they were there, Timothy joined them as they revisited the congregations in that area (Acts 16:1-5). They continued their journey to the west and considered going into Asia and to Bithynia, but the Holy Spirit told them not to go that way (Acts 16:6-7). So, they traveled to Troas where Paul had a vision of a man saying, "Come over to Macedonia and help us" (Acts 16:8-9).

Now after he had seen the vision, immediately we sought to go to Macedonia, concluding that the Lord had called us to preach the gospel to them (Acts 16:10).

Since Luke wrote "we sought" and "called us to preach," shows us that he joined this three-man team. It also suggests that he was a preacher and was possibly preaching at the Troas church (Acts 20:6; 2 Cor. 2:12). These four men boarded a boat and made their way to Philippi (Acts 16:11-12).

Philippi was a city built on a plain surrounded by mountains. It was located in the eastern part of Macedonia and it was named after Philip II, which was the father of Alexander the Great, in 356 B.C.

> In 42 B.C., Mark Antony and Octavian (later Augustus Caesar) combined forces to defeat the armies of Brutus and Cassius, assassins of Julius Caesar, at Philippi. In celebration of the victory, Philippi was made into a Roman colony; this entitled its inhabitants to the rights and privileges usually granted those who lived in Italy" (Nelson's New Illustrated Bible 984).

Since Philippi was honored as a Roman colony, that is probably what is meant by Philippi being "the foremost city of that part of Macedonia" (Acts 16:12).

And on the Sabbath day we went out of the city to the riverside, where prayer was customarily made; and we sat down and spoke to the women who met *there* (Acts 16:13).

On Saturday, these men made their way to the river one mile west of town, which is believed to be the Gangites River. According to the Rabbis, it took ten Jewish men to have a synagogue. Apparently, there were not enough Jewish men in Philippi to have a synagogue. One possible reason for this shortage of Jewish men was because Claudius had banned the Jews from Rome, which would have included their colonies like Philippi (Acts 18:2). When there was not a Synagogue, the Jews would customarily meet by a river or a source of water so there would be plenty of water available for their ceremonial washings.

Archeology offers another possible reason these Jews met at the river outside the city.

> French excavations at Philippi between 1914 and 1938 unearthed a Roman arch that lay about one mile west of the city. This arch may have served as a zoning marker to restrict undesirable religious sects from meeting in the city (Nelson's New Illustrated Bible 984).

Next, we learn that these four men sat down and spoke to these women.

Now a certain woman named Lydia heard *us*. She was a seller of purple from the city of Thyatira, who worshiped God. The Lord opened her heart to heed the things spoken by Paul (Acts 16:14).

Lydia was either a Jew or a proselyte. Since she was a seller of purple, she was probably well-off because this color was sought after by the rich, and it was expensive.

> The dye itself was derived from the murex shellfish found in the Mediterranean Sea. A total of 250,000 mollusks were required to make one ounce of the dye, which partly accounts for its great price (Nelson's New Illustrated Bible 288).

It is interesting that Paul and his companions were not allowed to go into Asia, yet Lydia was from Asia. "Thyatira was a wealthy town in the northern part of Lydia of the Roman province of Asia, on the river Lycus" (ISBE). It was also the home of one of the seven churches mentioned in the book of Revelation (Rev. 2:18). Thyatira was known for having guilds, and one of those guilds was selling purple dye. Lydia would have belonged to this guild because a person had to be a member of it to get the dye and be allowed to sell it.

Those who teach the false doctrine of Calvinism will use this verse to teach that the Holy Spirit must directly operate on the sinner before the Word of God will have any power or influence on them. Therefore, they would say the only reason Lydia listened to the Word of God and became saved was because God directly opened her heart with the Holy Spirit and made His grace irresistible.

However, there is nothing in the Scriptures that justifies this teaching. I have already pointed out in the eunuch's and Cornelius's conversion that the Holy Spirit does not directly teach or involve Himself with the conversion of a sinner. Instead, He would direct a preacher to that sinner so they could hear the words that would save them (Acts 11:14). After all, God's Word is the power of God to salvation (Rom. 1:16), and when we receive it, it will save our soul (Jam. 1:21). God draws us and calls us through His Word (Jn. 6:44-45; 2 Thes. 2:14). As Paul said: "How then shall they call on Him in whom they have not believed? And how shall they believe in Him of whom they have not heard? And how shall they hear without a preacher?" (Rom. 10:14). Then Paul said: "So then faith *comes* by hearing, and hearing by the word of God" (Rom. 10:17).

Since we have to have faith to be pleasing to God (Heb. 11:6), and faith comes from hearing the Word of God; this proves the Holy Spirit does not directly cause us to have faith. Instead, the Holy Spirit instructs us indirectly through the Word of God because it is the sword of the Spirit (Eph. 6:17), which means we have to choose to allow it to open up our heart.

In Saul's conversion, Jesus instructed him to be a witness for Him so he could open the eyes of the people (Acts 26:16-18), which is equivalent to opening up their hearts, and it was done by preaching the truth. That is how the Lord opened Lydia's heart. Lydia was already seeking after God because she worshipped Him and prayed to Him. Lydia would have been receptive to hearing things about God, so she listened to what these men had to say, and it was through their message that God opened her heart and drew her in.

And when she and her household were baptized, she begged *us,* saying, "If you have judged me to be faithful to the Lord, come to my house and stay." So she persuaded us (Acts 16:15).

We are not specifically told what Paul and these other men taught these women, but we can know they taught them about Jesus and what they needed to do to be saved. We can also know their teaching included baptism because she and her household were baptized. Most likely they were baptized in the river that was there. This conversion marks the beginning of a new congregation in Philippi. These Christians at Philippi would become a constant source of joy for Paul as we learn from the book of Philippians. Since Lydia is not mentioned in the book of Philippians, it is possible that she either died or was no longer in Philippi when Paul wrote that letter. Lydia showed her hospitality and persuaded these men to stay at her house for awhile.

Those who teach infant baptism will appeal to verses like these. They will claim there could have been an infant in her household, and it would have been baptized as well. However, there is nothing in the Scriptures that supports this doctrine. There is no need for an infant to be baptized because he is innocent of sin (Mt. 18:1-4); he also cannot believe or obey the commands of God. A person's household would include his slaves and his family, but there is nothing in our text that hints at Lydia being married or having children. Since her household could hear the message being taught, believe it,

107

and obey it by being baptized, the evidence is that there were no infants in her household.

Similar arguments can be made for the other instances of households that were baptized. For instance, the household of Cornelius feared God (Acts 10:2), heard the words spoken (Acts 10:33, 44), spoke in tongues (Acts 10:46), and could be commanded (Acts 10:48). The Philippian jailer's household was baptized, and they could hear the words that were spoken to them, believe, and rejoice (Acts 16:31-34). Stephanas' household was baptized (1 Cor. 1:16), and they could devote themselves to the ministry of the saints (1 Cor. 16:15). Since infants cannot do any of these things, it proves that these households did not have any.

As these men stayed in Philippi, they continued to go to the place of prayer. A slave girl, possessed by a spirit of divination, kept following them and saying: "These men are the servants of the Most High God, who proclaim to us the way of salvation" (Acts 16:16-17). It is interesting how these demons always spoke the truth about Jesus' identity, and they recognized those who belonged to Him and preached His Word (Mt. 8:29; Mk. 1:24; 3:11; Lk. 4:41; 8:28; Acts 19:13-17). This demon had given this slave girl the ability to tell the future, and her owners were making money from this ability. From the Greek, this spirit was known as the Python Spirit.

Gareeth Reese writes:

> In Greek mythology, Python was a monstrous dragon who lived in a cave on Mt. Parnassus just north of the town of Delphi in Greece. In the town of Delphi was a temple where people could get their fortunes told. The place had long been a center of pagan worship, whose priest had developed an elaborate ritual, centered about a chief priestess whose

title was Pythia. Kings and public officials would come to get their fortunes told and to get advice on matters of national policy, and private citizens would come to seek information about marriage or business ventures. The Python was supposed to give them the advice they sought. It worked in this fashion. In the center of the temple at Delphi was a small opening in the ground from whence mind-bending fumes arose. The priestess breathed these, sat down on a three-legged stool located over the opening, and thence delivered the "oracles." Having breathed the fumes, the priestess became violently agitated, and spoke in tongues (frenzied, ecstatic syllabication) whatever the Python prompted her to say. A poet or priest standing by would then "translate" what the Pythoness had said and give the "prophecy" to the worshipper who had come to inquire of the Oracle at Delphi…. Actually, according to Greek mythology, Apollo (the son of Zeus) had long ago slain the dragon, and himself took over giving these revelations. But the priestesses were still commonly said to be possessed by a Python spirit (Reese 580).

Knowing this background information teaches us the reason this particular Greek word was used because this slave girl was possessed by a spirit that had the same characteristics credited to the priestess of Delphi. There is no proof that this demon could predict the future. Most likely it was just good at deceiving those who were gullible enough to believe what it said.

Paul grew tired of the demon saying the same thing day after day, so he cast it out of the slave girl in the name of Jesus

Christ (Acts 16:18), which made her owners angry because they would no longer be able to make money off her ability. So, they dragged Paul and Silas before the authorities and accused them of teaching things that were against Roman law. (Acts 16:18-21). These false accusations made all the people angry, and the magistrates stripped them of their clothing and beat them with rods (Acts 16:22-23). When the Jews would beat someone, they gave them forty stripes minus one (2 Cor. 11:24; Deut. 25:2-3), but there was no such limit with a Roman beating. They were beaten with rods about the size of a broom handle, and since there was no limit, sometime people died from these beatings. There was no formal investigation of these accusations, and Paul considered this a shameful act by these people (1 Thes. 2:2).

After they beat them, they threw them into the inner prison (third compartment). In a Roman prison, there were usually three distinct parts:

1. The communiora, which allowed the prisoner to have light and fresh air.
2. The Interiora, an area shut off by strong iron gates with bars and locks.
3. The tullianium or dungeon, a place of execution or for one condemned to die (Boles 261).

They also put their feet in stocks, which were a form of restraint and torture. They were made from "a log or timber with holes in which the feet, hands, neck of prisoners were inserted and fastened with thongs" (Thayer). The text points out that only their feet were bound. Typically the stocks would hold the prisoners legs so far apart that it caused them pain, and it made it almost impossible for them to stand.

But at midnight Paul and Silas were praying and singing hymns to God, and the prisoners were listening to them (Acts 16:25).

This was an amazing display of how much trust Paul and Silas had in God. They did not complain to God or ask Him why they had to suffer this way. Instead, they prayed and sung to the Lord. Grammatically from the Greek, this was one act; so they were singing their prayers to God. As A.T. Robertson said:

> Were praying and singing (*proseuchomenoi hum-noun*). Present middle participle and imperfect active indicative: Praying they were singing (simultaneously, blending together petition and praise).

As Christians, we should learn to match their faithfulness in our times of distress. When we compare our troubles to theirs, we will realize that our troubles are mild. As they sang and prayed to God at midnight, the other prisoners were listening to them, and so was God.

Suddenly there was a great earthquake, so that the foundations of the prison were shaken; and immediately all the doors were opened and everyone's chains were loosed. And the keeper of the prison, awaking from sleep and seeing the prison doors open, supposing the prisoners had fled, drew his sword and was about to kill himself. But Paul called with a loud voice, saying, "Do yourself no harm, for we are all here" (Acts 16:26-28).

Those who try to dismiss this event as being from God will say this was just a coincidence because Philippi is known for having earthquakes. However, we can see this was a precise earthquake as it did not cause the roof to fall in, and it shook the prison just enough to knock the doors opens and break the chains free from the wall. God caused a similar earthquake in Acts 4:31.

This event woke up the jailer, and when he saw the doors were open, he assumed the prisoners had escaped. So, he drew his sword and was going to kill himself. Roman jailers were punished by death if they allowed prisoners to escape, and it was common for them to take their own life instead of facing a torturous death at the hands of the Romans. Paul knew what this man was about to do; so he yelled out to him to keep him from taking his own life.

Then he called for a light, ran in, and fell down trembling before Paul and Silas. And he brought them out and said, "Sirs, what must I do to be saved?" So they said, "Believe on the Lord Jesus Christ, and you will be saved, you and your household." Then they spoke the word of the Lord to him and to all who were in his house. And he took them the same hour of the night and washed *their* stripes. And immediately he and all his family were baptized. Now when he had brought them into his house, he set food before them; and he rejoiced, having believed in God with all his household (Acts 16:29-34).

Even though it is not mentioned in the text, the jailer probably secured the other prisoners first so that they would not escape, and then he fell before Paul and Silas. The jailer's action suggests that he associated this event as being from the God that Paul and Silas had been singing and praying to. This association would be made stronger if he was told how Paul had cast the demon out of the slave girl earlier. After the jailer fell down before them trembling, he brought them out of the jail, and he wanted to know what he must do to be saved, which implies that he was told what the slave girl had said about them: "These men are the servants of the Most High God, who proclaim to us the way of salvation" (Acts 16:17-18). So, they said: "Believe on the Lord Jesus Christ, and you will be saved, you and your household." Those who teach the "faith only" doctrine appeal to these verses as a prooftext.

However, this text does not teach what they want it to because simply believing in Jesus will not save a person (Jam. 2:24); it requires an obedient faith (Heb. 5:8-9).

As J.W. McGarvey once wrote:

> Those who argue that the jailer obtained pardon by faith alone, leave the jail too soon. If they would remain one hour longer, they would see him immersed for the remission of his sins, and rejoicing in the knowledge of pardon after his immersion, not before it.

When they told the jailer to believe on Jesus, they were using the word *believe* as a synecdoche because believing on the Lord includes all that is necessary for salvation including baptism. We cannot exclude God's grace, repentance, confession, or baptism from the plan of salvation because all these things are necessary to be saved (Eph. 2:8; Lk. 13:3; Rom. 10:9-10; 1 Pet. 3:21). This conversion teaches us that more than mere belief in Jesus was involved because Paul and Silas spoke the Word of God to the jailer's household, which they had to hear to be saved (Acts 11:14).

After Paul and Silas preached to them, the jailer took these men in the middle of the night and washed their stripes. When he finished, the jailer and his household were immediately baptized. Not only does this reaffirm that baptism was done in water, it also shows the urgency of being baptized. If baptism was just an outward sign for an inward change, why would this family get baptized in the middle of the night? The answer is obvious: their baptism was for the remission of sins (Acts 2:38; 22:16), and they understood they would be lost until they submitted themselves to it. Just like the Ethiopian eunuch, they did not rejoice until after they had been baptized.

The following verse also proves that believing on the Lord includes baptism:

Then Crispus, the ruler of the synagogue, believed on the Lord with all his household. And many of the Corinthians, hearing, believed and were baptized (Acts 18:8).

The Corinthians heard the Word, believed, and were baptized, but our text just says that Crispus "believed on the Lord with all his household." Does this mean that Crispus and his household merely believed in Jesus? No, because when we consider the whole counsel of God, we learn that believing on the Lord includes baptism. Paul said, "I thank God that I baptized none of you except Crispus and Gaius" (1 Cor. 1:14). Again, this fact proves that baptism is included in believing on the Lord.

The third conversion we will examine happened during Paul's third missionary journey as he made his way into Ephesus.

And it happened, while Apollos was at Corinth, that Paul, having passed through the upper regions, came to Ephesus. And finding some disciples he said to them, "Did you receive the Holy Spirit when you believed?" So they said to him, "We have not so much as heard whether there is a Holy Spirit. And he said to them, "Into what then were you baptized?" So they said, "Into John's baptism" (Acts 19:1-3).

Since we are missing some details in these verses, we are forced to speculate on some things. Paul finds some disciples as he comes to Ephesus, but whose disciples are they? We need to remember that a disciple simply means a learner or a pupil. At this point, we cannot tell if Paul suspects they are Christians or non-Christians. There are two possible reasons

Paul asked them, "Did you receive the Holy Spirit when you believed?"

First, he may have suspected or even knew they were not Christians, and he knew this question would confirm whose disciples they were and if they knew about the giving of the Holy Spirit.

Second, if he thought they were Christians, he may have asked this question to find out if they had received the miraculous gifts of the Holy Spirit through the hands of an apostle. If not, he could impart these miraculous gifts to them.

No matter what Paul's intentions were with this question, it revealed that these men only knew John's baptism, and they had not heard about the giving of the Holy Spirit.

Then Paul said, "John indeed baptized with a baptism of repentance, saying to the people that they should believe on Him who would come after him, that is, on Christ Jesus." When they heard *this,* they were baptized in the name of the Lord Jesus (Acts 19:4-5).

John's baptism was temporary, and it was only valid until the death of Jesus on the cross. After Jesus was raised from the dead with all power and authority, He commanded that baptism was to be done in the name of the Father, the Son, and the Holy Spirit (Mt. 28:19). As revealed by Peter, baptism is for the remission of sins, and it is the time when we receive the gift of the Holy Spirit (Acts 2:38). It is also when we are added to the church by God (Acts 2:47) and put into Christ (Rom. 6:3; Gal. 3:27).

When these disciples found out that John's baptism was no longer valid, they realized they needed to believe on Jesus, which I have already shown includes the entire plan of salvation. That is the reason they were baptized in the name of the Lord Jesus.

This conversion also teaches us that we must understand what we are being baptized into. So, if we were baptized for the wrong reason, then we need to be baptized for the right reason. For instance, if we were baptized as an infant, our baptism is invalid because we did not believe, repent, or confess, since these are impossible for an infant to do. If we were taught that baptism was an outward sign for inward change and we were "saved" before baptism, then we could not have been baptized for the remission of sins (Acts 2:38), which makes our baptism invalid. If we were baptized to join a man-made denomination, then we did not understand that baptism puts us into Christ and that God adds us to His church. It is critical that we examine the reason we were baptized. If we discover that we were not baptized into Christ for the remission of our sins, then we need to follow the example of these twelve men and be baptized in accordance with God's will.

And when Paul had laid hands on them, the Holy Spirit came upon them, and they spoke with tongues and prophesied (Acts 19:6).

Just like the conversion of the Samaritans, these men were baptized in the name of Jesus. Then Paul laid his hands on them so they could receive the miraculous gifts of the Holy Spirit, which gave them the ability to speak in tongues and prophesy.

In conclusion, these three conversions Paul was involved with have remained consistent with all the other conversions. Once again, they confirm that we must hear about Jesus, believe in Him, repent, confess Him, and be baptized for the remission of sins. Finally, these conversions do not offer any support for the false doctrines of infant baptism, "faith only," or the Calvinistic view of the Holy Spirit directly operating on the heart of a sinner, making God's grace irresistible.

Questions

1. Discuss Lydia's background.
2. How was Lydia's heart opened to the truth?
3. Can babies be scripturally baptized?
4. Discuss the demon possessed slave girl.
5. Was the Philippian jailor taught that he could be saved by faith alone?
6. Why was the Philippian jailor's household baptized in the middle of the night?
7. What do we learn about baptism from the conversion of the former disciples of John in Acts 19?

BURIED WITH CHRIST
Romans 6

9

In Romans 6, Paul gives a detailed description of what happens when we are baptized in water. This chapter is full of rich information that will prove that baptism is absolutely necessary for salvation. In the previous chapter, Paul taught the Romans they were justified by an obedient faith to God and that justification comes through Jesus. Even though we are all sinners (Rom. 3:23), grace, which came through Christ (Jn. 1:17), will always have the power to overcome our sins. Again, this requires an obedient faith (Heb. 5:8-9; 1 Jn. 1:7).

What shall we say then? Shall we continue in sin that grace may abound? Certainly not! How shall we who died to sin live any longer in it? (Rom. 6:1-2).

Grace is not designed to be a safety net in which we are allowed to sin freely. Grace can be perverted (Jude 1:4), and we can fall from it (Gal. 5:4). Notice how firm Paul answered his own question. He said, "Certainly not!" He wanted them to understand this truth because some had been twisting what he had been teaching.

And *why* not *say,* "Let us do evil that good may come"? -- as we are slanderously reported and as some affirm that we say (Rom. 3:8).

119

So, Paul put the rumors to rest; grace is not a license to sin. His next question is an important one. "How shall we who died to sin live any longer in it?" Later, we will see that a person is either a servant of sin or a servant or righteousness. If a person is a servant of righteousness, then he is a Christian and he has died to sin, which means he should do his best to never become a servant of sin again.

When we become a Christian, we die to sin, but the temptation to sin is still there. So, we must continue to stay away from sin. Once we die to sin, we should rejoice because we have overcome sin and are no longer separated from God (Rom. 6:23; Isa. 59:2). So, we must die to sin if we ever hope to be saved.

How and when do we die to sin? Paul answered this question in the following verses:

Or do you not know that as many of us as were baptized into Christ Jesus were baptized into His death? Therefore we were buried with Him through baptism into death, that just as Christ was raised from the dead by the glory of the Father, even so we also should walk in newness of life (Rom. 6:3-4).

In Him you were also circumcised with the circumcision made without hands, by putting off the body of the sins of the flesh, by the circumcision of Christ, buried with Him in baptism, in which you also were raised with *Him* through faith in the working of God, who raised Him from the dead (Col. 2:11-12).

We can learn several things from these verses:

1. Baptism is what puts us into Christ. Paul taught the same thing to the Galatians: "For as many of you as were baptized *into Christ* have put on Christ" (Gal. 3:27, emph. mine). So,

being baptized into Christ means a person has clothed himself with Him. To show the significance of being in Christ, notice the following things that are found in Christ:

- Every spiritual blessing (Eph. 1:3).
- Forgiveness of sin (Eph. 1:7).
- No condemnation (Rom. 8:2).
- New creation (2 Cor. 5:17).
- Grace (2 Tim. 2:1).
- Salvation (2 Tim. 2:10).
- Eternal life (1 Jn. 5:11).

Obviously, if we want to be saved and possess all these things found in Christ, we need to be put into and clothed with Christ. None of these benefits are found outside Christ. Paul taught that baptism is how we get into Christ where all these wonderful blessings are found. If we have not been baptized into Christ, then we are lost.

2. Paul pointed out that baptism is the point we die with Christ, which is not a physical death, but a spiritual one. He also pointed out that baptism is a burial, which fits perfectly with the definition of baptism from the Greek: "*To dip repeatedly, to immerse, submerge* (of vessels sunk)" (Thayer). This definition describes exactly what happens when we are lowered under the water because we are completely immersed, which emulates being buried with Christ. Since we are the ones that are being immersed and buried, this rules out sprinkling or pouring. Besides, sprinkling (*rhantismos*) and pouring (*ballo, epicheo*) have their own Greek words, and they have nothing to do with the meaning of baptism (*baptizo*).

Another way to illustrate this definition is by giving an example that we will all agree on. When a person passes away and he is buried in the graveyard, do we pour or sprinkle a little dirt on him and call him buried? Of course not! Everyone understands that buried means he is completely covered with dirt, which is the same idea we are given with baptism. Since baptism is a burial in water, John was baptizing where there was much water (Jn. 3:23), and Philip and the eunuch went into the water (Acts 8:38).

3. Another interesting point comes from the word *buried*, which is the Greek word *sunthapto*. This Greek word only occurs two times in the Bible (Rom. 6:4; Col. 2:12). Notice how this word is defined and viewed by the following Lexicons:

> *Bury (together) with* or *at the same time*; figuratively, of identifying with Christ through baptism in accepting his death and burial as one's own (RO 6.4) (Friberg).

> To bury someone along with someone else - 'to bury together with.' 'by our baptism, then, we were buried with him and shared in his death' Ro 6.4 (Louw-Nida).

> Of the believers being buried together with their Lord in baptism (BDAG).

> *To bury together with*: together with Christ, passive, namely, Rom. 6:4; Col. 2:12. For all who in the rite of baptism are plunged under the water thereby declare that they put faith in the expiatory death of Christ for the pardon of their past sins; therefore Paul likens baptism to a burial by which the former sinfulness is buried, i.e. utterly taken away (Thayer).

122

Even A.T. Robertson, renowned Baptist Greek scholar, who taught that baptism was not necessary for salvation agreed with Thayer:

> Thayer's Lexicon says: "For all who in the rite of baptism are plunged under the water, thereby declare that they put faith in the expiatory death of Christ for the pardon of their past sins." Yes, and for all future sins also. This word gives Paul's vivid picture of baptism as a symbolic burial with Christ and resurrection also to newness of life in him as Paul shows by the addition "wherein ye were also raised with him". In the symbol of baptism the resurrection to new life in Christ is pictured with an allusion to Christ's own resurrection and to our final resurrection (Robertson).

Mr. Robertson admitted that water baptism is what Paul is talking about. He also admits that it is the point at which we are buried with Christ, which is the point our sins are taken away. However, as he continued, he tried to justify his belief, which contradicts what he just said:

> Paul does not mean to say that the new life in Christ is caused or created by the act of baptism. That is grossly to misunderstand him. The Gnostics and the Judaizers were sacramentalists, but not so Paul the champion of spiritual Christianity. He has just given the spiritual interpretation to circumcision which itself followed Abraham's faith (Ro 4:10-12). Cf. Gal 3:27. Baptism gives a picture of the change already wrought in the heart "through faith" (Robertson).

A.T. Robertson had a great understanding of the Greek language. However, he admitted in his massive Historical Grammar book that sometimes grammar must give way to theology (Jackson, *The Preposition "Eis" in Acts 2:38* www.christiancourier.com).

In other words, no matter how clear the Bible teaches that baptism is necessary for salvation, Robertson was willing to ignore it so he could hold to his Baptist doctrine. Every time the Scriptures talk about the necessity of baptism, Robertson tried to explain it away. Based on these Greek Lexicons and the Bible, we can see that Paul was teaching that being baptized in water is necessary for our salvation.

4. Paul confirmed that baptism is the point at which we die to our sins because we are buried with Christ in His death. Paul compared baptism to circumcision. Under the Law of Moses, a male child had to be physically circumcised on the 8th day to enter the covenant made by God (Lev. 12:3). However, under the new covenant, both men and women are spiritually circumcised when they are baptized. At that point, they enter the covenant made by God. The word *circumcised* has the basic meaning of being cut off, and that is what happens to us in baptism because our sins are cut off from us. Paul will make this point even stronger when we examine verse 5 and following.

5. Paul taught that baptism is not a work of man, but a work of God. However, it is a response on our part in the sense that we decide to submit to water baptism. However, what happens at our baptism is done solely by God, which can be proven in several ways:

(1) Every time the Word of God speaks of someone being baptized, it is always in the passive tense, which means baptism is something that is being done to us. Someone might

say this is referring to the person who is baptizing the other person. However, we need to realize that when a person is helping another person with his baptism, he is simply making sure that person is fully immersed because that person has nothing to do with the work that happens to the person being baptized.

(2) Paul said: "Buried with Him in baptism, in which you also were raised with *Him through faith in the working of God*, who raised Him from the dead" (Col. 2:12, emph. mine). Notice, it is by our faith in the working of God that we can know God is causing us to die to our sins and that He is uniting us with Christ in baptism. It is at the point of baptism that God adds us to His church (Acts 2:47), which is only something God can do. There is nothing magical about the water itself. It is simply the place that God has appointed in which we contact the saving blood of Jesus (Rev. 1:5) and our sins are washed away (Acts 2:38; 22:16; 1 Cor. 6:9-11).

(3) This idea can be seen in the Old Testament as well. In 2 Kings 5, we learn about a commander of the Syrian army named Naaman. He was a successful military leader, but he had leprosy. His king wanted him to be healed, so he sent a letter to the king of Israel to let him know he was sending Naaman to him to be healed. The king of Israel could not help him with this request, but Elisha could. So, Naaman was sent to Elisha's house and Elisha sent a servant out to tell him: "Go and wash in the Jordan seven times, and your flesh shall be restored to you, and *you shall* be clean" (2 Kgs. 5:10). At first, Naaman was furious, and he refused, but his servant talked him into obeying Elisha's command, and he was cleansed of his leprosy. There was nothing magical about the Jordan River, but it was the place that Elisha said he would be healed from his leprosy. It was not until he obeyed that command and dipped seven times that God cleansed him from his leprosy. Again, the water itself did not cure him, just like the water itself does not wash away our sins. Instead, it is

the working of God combined with an obedient faith that healed Naaman and causes us to have the forgiveness of our sins.

6. Once we have been baptized into Christ and we are raised from the watery grave of baptism, we are supposed "to walk in newness of life." Notice, our walk in newness of life does not begin until we are buried with Christ in baptism. Paul said: "Therefore, if anyone *is* in Christ, *he is* a new creation; old things have passed away; behold, all things have become new" (2 Cor. 5:17). Again, the only way we can become a new creation is by being baptized into Christ.

For if we have been united together in the likeness of His death, certainly we also shall be *in the likeness* of *His* resurrection, knowing this, that our old man was crucified with *Him,* that the body of sin might be done away with, that we should no longer be slaves of sin. For he who has died has been freed from sin (Rom. 6:5-7).

And you, being dead in your trespasses and the uncircumcision of your flesh, He has made alive together with Him, having forgiven you all trespasses (Col. 2:13).

As Paul continued, he lets us know that our salvation and the forgiveness of our sins are conditional. Verse 5 starts out with the Greek word *gar*, which means Paul was explaining more about what he said in the previous verse. Notice the conditional word *if.* We can only be united with Christ in the likeness of His death if we are baptized. It is at the point of baptism that our old self is crucified with Christ. At that point, we are freed from our sins and made alive with Christ by our faith in the working of God. Paul said: "I have been crucified with Christ; it is no longer I who live, but Christ lives in me; and the *life* which I now live in the flesh I live by faith in the Son of God, who loved me and gave Himself for me" (Gal.

2:20). It was only when Paul was crucified with Christ in baptism that Christ lived in him (Acts 9:18).

Just because we have been freed from our past sins does not mean that we cannot sin any more. Instead, it means that we should not sin any more. It is also important to note, that once we have been baptized into Christ for the remission of our sins, we do not need to be baptized every time we sin. Instead, we have been given the privilege to come boldly before the throne of grace in prayer to repent and confess our sins to God (Heb. 4:16; 1 Jn. 1:9). Consider the following verses:

If then you were raised with Christ, seek those things which are above, where Christ is, sitting at the right hand of God. Set your mind on things above, not on things on the earth. For you died, and your life is hidden with Christ in God. When Christ _who is_ our life appears, then you also will appear with Him in glory. Therefore put to death your members which are on the earth: fornication, uncleanness, passion, evil desire, and covetousness, which is idolatry. Because of these things the wrath of God is coming upon the sons of disobedience, in which you yourselves once walked when you lived in them. But now you yourselves are to put off all these: anger, wrath, malice, blasphemy, filthy language out of your mouth. Do not lie to one another, since you have put off the old man with his deeds, and have put on the new _man_ who is renewed in knowledge according to the image of Him who created him, where there is neither Greek nor Jew, circumcised nor uncircumcised, barbarian, Scythian, slave _nor_ free, but Christ _is_ all and in all (Col. 3:1-11, see also Eph. 4:20ff).

Once again, we have the conditional word _if_. Paul is saying, if we were raised with Christ in baptism, we should be seeking those things which are above. When he said, "you died," he is referring to when we died in baptism, which was when our life became hidden with Christ. It is only when we have died and been raised with Christ in baptism that we have the hope of appearing with Jesus when He appears at His second coming. Then Paul encourages us to put off all these sinful deeds that cause us to be separated from God. He tells us why we should do this when he wrote, "…since you have put off the old man with his deeds, and have put on the new *man* who is renewed in knowledge according to the image of Him who created him" (Col. 3:9-10). Again, Paul teaches us in Romans 6 that putting off the old man happens at the point of baptism. Paul told Titus: "This is a faithful saying: For if we died with Him, We shall also live with Him" (2 Tim. 2:11). Notice, the only way we can live with Christ is by dying with Him, which happens at the point of baptism.

Now if we died with Christ, we believe that we shall also live with Him, knowing that Christ, having been raised from the dead, dies no more. Death no longer has dominion over Him. For *the death* that He died, He died to sin once for all; but *the life* that He lives, He lives to God. Likewise you also, reckon yourselves to be dead indeed to sin, but alive to God in Christ Jesus our Lord (Rom. 6:8-11).

Verse 8 is the same conditional statement that Paul made to Timothy (2 Tim. 2:11). We can know with all confidence that if we die with Christ in baptism and we remain faithful, we will live with Christ in heaven forever. We can know this fact because Jesus was raised from the dead, and He has put sin in its place. Just as Jesus lives for God, we are supposed to live our lives for God and consider ourselves dead to sin but alive in Jesus.

Therefore do not let sin reign in your mortal body, that you should obey it in its lusts. And do not present your members *as* instruments of unrighteousness to sin, but present yourselves to God as being alive from the dead,

and your members *as* instruments of righteousness to God. For sin shall not have dominion over you, for you are not under law but under grace (Rom. 6:12-14).

This passage proves we can resist sin. However, we are human and sometimes we will sin (1 Jn. 1:8, 10), which is why Paul taught us not to let sin reign in our bodies. As Christians, we are to fight the good fight of faith (1 Tim. 6:12) and keep sin out of our lives (1 Jn. 2:15-17; 3:9; 1:6). When Paul said: "We are not under law but under grace," he is saying that we are not under the Law of Moses in which perfect law-keeping was required. "For whoever shall keep the whole law, and yet stumble in one *point,* he is guilty of all" (James 2:10). Some seem to think there is no law under the system of grace, but this is not true. Consider the following proof:

Isaiah prophesied that the law of Jehovah would go forth from Jerusalem (Isa. 2:3), which happened on the day of Pentecost (Acts 2). When the new covenant was made through Jesus, Jeremiah prophesied that God would put His law in their minds and write it on their hearts (Jer. 31:33). The fact that we are under a new covenant proves that we are under a law, and the Scriptures make it clear that we are under a law. For instance, the covenant we are under is called a law of faith (Rom. 3:27), the law of God (Rom. 7:22, 25), and the law of the Spirit of life (Rom. 8:2). Paul said he was under law to Christ (1 Cor. 9:21), and he taught other Christians to fulfill the law of Christ (Gal. 6:2). James called it the perfect law of liberty and the royal law (James 1:25; 2:8, 12). Besides, if there is no law, then there is no way we can sin (Rom. 4:15). However, Jesus said: "If you love Me, keep My commandments" (Jn. 14:15). If there are commandments we can keep, then there is a law for us to keep. There are many other verses that show that we must obey God's law under His system of grace as well (Mt. 7:21-23; Rom. 6:17-18; Col. 3:5-6; 2 Thes. 1:8-9; Heb. 5:8-9; James 1:22; 2:17, 20; 1 Pet. 4:17; 1 Jn. 2:3-4, 17; 5:3; 1 Pet. 1:22; Rev. 21:7-8; 22:14).

What then? Shall we sin because we are not under law but under grace? Certainly not! Do you not know that to whom you present yourselves slaves to obey, you are that one's slaves whom you obey, whether of sin *leading* to death, or of obedience *leading* to righteousness? But God be thanked that *though* you were slaves of sin, yet you obeyed from the heart that form of doctrine to which you were delivered. And having been set free from sin, you became slaves of righteousness. I speak in human *terms* because of the weakness of your flesh. For just as you presented your members *as* slaves of uncleanness, and of lawlessness *leading* to *more* lawlessness, so now present your members *as* slaves *of* righteousness for holiness (Rom. 6:15-19).

Once again, Paul is teaching us that grace is not a license to sin. When we were baptized into Christ, we made ourselves slaves of righteousness. We are no longer supposed to be slaves of sin because it leads to spiritual death. Notice how they became slaves of righteousness, which caused them to be set free from sin. They obeyed from the heart that form of doctrine that was delivered to them. What doctrine was delivered to them that they obeyed? It was the same doctrine that Jesus told His disciples to teach in The Great Commission (Mt. 28:19-20; Mk. 16:15-16). When they went around teaching, they taught that a person must believe that Jesus is the Son of God (Jn. 8:24; Acts 8:37), repent (Lk. 13:3; Acts 2:38), confess Jesus as Lord (Mt. 10:32-33; Rom. 10:9-10), and be baptized (Mk. 16:16; Acts 2:38). Paul continued to encourage these brethren to be servants of righteousness.

For when you were slaves of sin, you were free in regard to righteousness. What fruit did you have then in the things of which you are now ashamed? For the end of those things *is* death. But now having been set free from sin, and having become slaves of God, you have your fruit to holiness, and the end, everlasting life. For the

wages of sin *is* death, but the gift of God *is* eternal life in Christ Jesus our Lord (Rom. 6:20-23).

As Paul summed up this chapter, he pointed out that being a slave of sin will end in spiritual death, but being a slave of righteousness will result in inheriting eternal life through Jesus our Lord.

In conclusion, Paul has taught us with clarity the necessity of baptism. When we are baptized into Christ, we die to sin and we become slaves of righteousness because we obeyed that form of doctrine that has been delivered to us. If we have not been baptized into Christ, then we are still a slave of sin. If we die physically in this condition, the Word of God teaches that we will not make it into heaven. What about you, dear reader? Are you a slave of righteousness or a slave of sin? If you desire to be a slave of righteousness, then why not be united with Christ in baptism today (2 Cor. 6:2)?

Questions

1. Does God's grace give us a license to sin?
2. Name six important things we learn about baptism from Romans 6:3-4 and Colossians 2:11-12.
3. After we are baptized, do we have to get rebaptized every time we sin?
4. What did Paul mean when he said, "We are not under law but under grace?"
5. How do we become a slave of righteousness?

Otherwise, what will they do who are baptized for the dead, if the dead do not rise at all? Why then are they baptized for the dead? (1 Cor. 15:29).

It has been said there are thirty to forty different interpretations of this text. For instance, the Mormon Church uses this text to teach the false doctrine of proxy baptism. Joseph Smith is the founder of this denomination. He claimed to receive a new revelation from God, and the book of Mormon was born. He also claimed that Paul was teaching that we can be baptized in place of another that has passed on so they can be saved.

According to H. David Burton:

> The first public affirmation of the ordinance of baptism for the dead in the Church was Joseph Smith's funeral sermon for Seymour Brunson in Nauvoo in August 1840. Addressing a widow who had lost a son who had not been baptized, he called the principle "glad tidings of great joy," in contrast to the prevailing tradition that all un-baptized are damned. The first baptisms for the dead in modern

times were done in the Mississippi River near Nauvoo ("Baptism for the Dead").

According to Joseph's doctrine, I could be baptized for my friends and loved ones that have died so they can be saved. However, the Scriptures do not support his view, nor does most of the religious world. This false doctrine is based on this one verse because no other verses in the Bible talk about being baptized for the dead. As we examine what Paul was talking about in this verse, we cannot make him contradict other clear passages on this topic, and we must examine the context of 1 Corinthians 15.

The first thing I want to prove is that Paul was not teaching that Christians could be baptized for the dead because this would contradict other clear passages, which teach that once a person dies, salvation cannot be obtained. Paul said:

For we must all appear before the judgment seat of Christ, that each one may receive the things *done* in the body, according to what he has done, whether good or bad (2 Cor. 5:10).

But why do you judge your brother? Or why do you show contempt for your brother? For we shall all stand before the judgment seat of Christ. For it is written: *"As I live, says the LORD, Every knee shall bow to Me, And every tongue shall confess to God. "So then each of us shall give account of himself to God (Rom. 14:10-12).

This same thought is seen in Romans 2:6, Revelation 20:12 and 22:12, which states that all will stand before Jesus and be judged based on what they have done whether it is good or bad. This is why Paul said: "…work out your own salvation with fear and trembling" (Phi. 2:12). We cannot be saved or lost by what somebody else does for us because we are accountable for what we do (Ezek.18:20), and there are no second chances because the writer of Hebrews said: "And as it is appointed for men to die once, but after this the judgment" (Heb. 9:27). These Scriptures prove that we must stand or fall by our own deeds, and no matter how many times we get baptized or do a good deed in the name of those that have passed away, it will not change their judgment.

Another great example that teaches against this false doctrine is the story of the rich man and Lazarus (Lk. 16:19-31). The rich man found himself in Hades, and Lazarus was in the bosom of Abraham. The rich man was in torment, and Lazarus was in comfort. The rich man cried out to Abraham and said: "Father Abraham, have mercy on me, and send Lazarus that he may dip the tip of his finger in water and cool my tongue; for I am tormented in this flame" (Lk. 16:24). The rich man wanted some relief, and this is understandable but notice Abraham's response:

But Abraham said, 'Son, remember that in your lifetime you received your good things, and likewise Lazarus evil things; but now he is comforted and you are tormented. And besides all this, between us and you there is a great gulf fixed, so that those who want to pass from here to you cannot, nor can those from there pass to us' (Lk. 16:25-26).

It is impossible for a person like the rich man or Lazarus to cross this great gulf. So, when we die, we are taken to one of these two places. If we did not obey the gospel, we will be where the rich man is. For the doctrine of proxy baptism to be true there would have to be a way for the sinner to cross this great gulf, but Jesus taught us that it cannot happen. Therefore, proxy baptism cannot be true.

It is also interesting that the Book of Mormon does not teach anything about baptizing the dead. Even though the Book of Mormon contradicts the Bible in many places, it agrees with the Bible in that we must repent before we are baptized, and it must be done while we are still living. Note the following verses from their book that teaches this principle:

> Yea, I would that ye would come forth and harden not your hearts any longer; for behold, now is the time and the day of your salvation; and therefore, if ye will repent and harden not your hearts, immediately shall the great plan of redemption be brought about unto you. For behold, this life is the time for men to prepare to meet God; yea, behold the day of this life is the day for men to perform their labors. And now, as I said unto you before, as ye have had so many witnesses, therefore, I beseech of you that ye do not procrastinate the day of your repentance until the end; for after this day of life, which is given us to prepare for eternity, behold, if we do not improve our time while in this life, then cometh the night of darkness wherein there can be no labor performed. Ye cannot say, when ye are brought to that awful crisis, that I will repent, that I will return to my God. Nay, ye cannot say this; for that same spirit which doth possess your bodies at the time that ye go out of this life, that same spirit will have power to possess your body in that eternal world. For behold, if ye have procrastinated the day of your repentance even until death, behold, ye have become subjected to the spirit of the devil, and he doth seal you his; therefore, the Spirit of the Lord hath withdrawn from you, and hath no place in you, and the devil hath all power over you; and this is the final state of the wicked (Alma 34: 31-35).

But behold, your days of probation are past; ye have procrastinated the day of your salvation until it is everlastingly too late, and your destruction is made sure; yea, for ye have sought all the days of your lives for that which ye could not obtain; and ye have sought for happiness in doing iniquity, which thing is contrary to the nature of that righteousness which is in our great and Eternal Head. O ye people of the land, that ye would hear my words! And I pray that the anger of the Lord be turned away from you, and that ye would repent and be saved (Helaman 13:38-39).

For behold that all little children are alive in Christ, and also all they that are without the law. For the power of redemption cometh on all them that have no law; wherefore, he that is not condemned, or he that is under no condemnation, cannot repent; and unto such baptism availeth nothing— But it is mockery before God, denying the mercies of Christ, and the power of his Holy Spirit, and putting trust in dead works (Moroni 8:22-23).

These verses from their book teach against the idea of proxy baptism. To find this false doctrine, we have to go to the Mormon's other book called *The Doctrine and Covenants of the Church of Jesus Christ of Latter-day Saints.*

This book is a collection of divine revelations and inspired declarations given for the establishment and regulation of the kingdom of God on the earth in the last days. Most of the revelations in this compilation were received through Joseph Smith, Jun., the first prophet and president of The Church of Jesus Christ of Latter-day Saints. Others were issued through some of his successors in the Presidency ("Explanatory Introduction The Doctrine and Covenants of the Church of Jesus Christ of Latter-day Saints").

This other book proves that Joseph Smith contradicts himself since the Book of Mormon, which he wrote, teaches against proxy baptism. God's Word and even the Book of Mormon show that Paul was not teaching the false doctrine of proxy baptism.

Now that we have ruled out proxy baptism, let us examine what Paul was talking about by examining the context of 1 Corinthians 15. This chapter is teaching us that Jesus was raised from the dead and that we will be raised from the dead. The reason Paul wrote this was to refute some false teachers that were saying there is no resurrection.

Now if Christ is preached that He has been raised from the dead, how do some among you say that there is no resurrection of the dead? (1 Cor. 15:12).

Some among you is referring to those who were teaching there is no resurrection of the dead. In verses 13 – 19, Paul teaches if there is no resurrection of the dead, then we are without hope, and Jesus has not risen. In verse 20 – 28, Paul affirms that Jesus was raised from the dead and that He is reigning over His kingdom right now. Just as Jesus was raised from the dead, we will be raised from dead. Then he asked several questions:

Otherwise, what will they do who are baptized for the dead, if the dead do not rise at all? Why then are they baptized for the dead? And why do we stand in jeopardy every hour? (1 Cor. 15:29-30).

All these questions are designed to show that if there is no resurrection, then there is no need for baptism or for putting your life in jeopardy. As Paul said, "If *the* dead do not rise, Let us eat and drink, for tomorrow we die" (1 Cor. 15:32). Then he warns these Christians not to keep company with these false teachers that are teaching there is no resurrection (1 Cor. 15:33). Paul continues teaching more about our bodily resurrection through the end of the chapter.

Now that we have examined the context, let us take a closer look at verse 29. First, we need to observe the pronouns. When Paul was speaking of himself or the Corinthians, he would use *I* or *you*. However, in our text, he used the word *they*, which is third person plural. So, he is not saying that he or the Christians at Corinth were baptizing for the dead. Instead, he is referring to the false teachers of verse 12. Those who were teaching there is no resurrection were being baptized for their dead. Paul was using an ad hominem argument (i.e., reasoning from your opponents' view) to show the fallacy of their false teaching. In other words, if there is no resurrection, there is no point in being baptized for the dead because when a person dies, it is all over.

An early writer named Tertullian (160 – 235 A.D.) believed there were some that practiced vicarious baptism at Corinth. Regarding baptizing for the dead, he wrote:

> Now it is certain that they adopted this (practice) with such a presumption as made them suppose that the vicarious baptism (in question) would be beneficial to the flesh of another in anticipation of the resurrection; for unless it were a bodily resurrection, there would be no pledge secured by this process of a corporeal baptism (*Ante-Nicene Fathers* Vol. 3 Resurrection of the Dead Explained Chapter XLVIII).

There should be no doubt that Paul was referring to these false teachers in this text. The only way this text could have applied to Paul or the Christians at Corinth is if Paul had said, "What will *we* do who are baptized for the dead?" Regarding these pronouns Burton Coffman wrote:

> Concerning Christian baptism, for example, it is always "we" or "you" who were baptized and addressed in the first or second persons, never in the third person. It is still "they" not "we" who baptize for the dead! (Coffman).

As I said earlier, there are 30 to 40 different interpretations of this verse, but I believe the one I have given is the most logical because it works well with the context, and it does not contradict any other teachings within the Word of God. One thing we know for sure, Paul was not teaching the false doctrine of proxy baptism. We should never try to build a new doctrine based off one ambiguous verse as the Mormons have done.

Questions

1. Discuss the Mormon's doctrine of proxy baptism.
2. After people die, can they still be saved?
3. What did Paul mean when he asked, "Why then are they baptized for the dead?"

For Christ also suffered once for sins, the just for the unjust, that He might bring us to God, being put to death in the flesh but made alive by the Spirit, by whom also He went and preached to the spirits in prison, who formerly were disobedient, when once the Divine longsuffering waited in the days of Noah, while *the* ark was being prepared, in which a few, that is, eight souls, were saved through water. There is also an antitype which now saves us -- baptism (not the removal of the filth of the flesh, but the answer of a good conscience toward God), through the resurrection of Jesus Christ, who has gone into heaven and is at the right hand of God, angels and authorities and powers having been made subject to Him (1 Pet. 3:18-22).

Peter is giving us a classic example of a type and antitype. The type is the salvation that Noah and his family received by water, and the antitype is our salvation by baptism in water that was made possible through Jesus' death and resurrection. We will examine this idea more in a minute, but first, let's deal with verses 18 – 20.

The first part of our passage is easy to understand because it is talking about how Jesus suffered for us on the cruel cross to become the perfect sacrifice for our sins. He did this because He loves us and wants us to be reconciled with God (Rom. 5:8-11). When Jesus was put to death in the flesh, He was raised alive by the Holy Spirit.

What Peter wrote next has caused the Catholic Church to teach the false doctrine of Purgatory, which does not exist anywhere in the Scriptures. They believe that Purgatory is a temporary place of punishment in which a person's soul is tormented for a certain length of time based on the sin he was guilty of. Once that time is up, they get to go to heaven. However, they claim that their priests can decrease that person's torment and get him into heaven quicker if they pray for them. In the middle ages, they made this into a money-making scheme and took advantage of their followers. This scheme was one of the problems that Martin Luther had with the Catholic Church. They continued to take advantage of their followers until Pope Pius V put an end to this practice in 1567. They still pray for the dead today, but they are not allowed to charge for it. Praying for the dead is not going to change anything because once a person dies his fate is sealed: "And as it is appointed for men to die once, but after this the judgment" (Heb. 9:27).

Some teach that when Jesus was dead for three days, His spirit went to the spirit realm, and He preached the gospel to those who died in the flood. Again, this interpretation would not make sense because their fates had already been sealed (Heb. 9:27); so it would be pointless for them to hear the gospel. Also, it would not make sense for Jesus to preach the gospel only to those spirits of Noah's day because that would be showing partiality, which God does not do (Acts 10:34). The story of the rich man and Lazarus in Luke 16 teaches us there are only two places we can go after we die. We either go to paradise, called Abraham's bosom, or we go to the place of torment, known as *tartarus* (2 Pet. 2:4). There is no escape from either of these places because the departed soul cannot cross the great gulf between these two places (Lk. 16:26).

Since we have ruled out Purgatory and Jesus preaching to the departed souls, let us find out what Peter is talking about.

First, we need find out when Jesus preached to these people. Peter answered this question by telling us that these spirits in prison, which refers to their location at the time Peter wrote this, were preached to during the time of Noah.

Second, we need to find out how Jesus preached to these people during Noah's day. Again, Peter answered this question earlier in his letter:

Of this salvation the prophets have inquired and searched carefully, who prophesied of the grace *that would come* to you, searching what, or what manner of time, the <u>Spirit of Christ who was in them</u> was indicating when He testified beforehand the sufferings of Christ and the glories that would follow (1 Pet. 1:10-11).

Notice, the spirit of Christ is said to have been in these prophets of old who were proclaiming God's Word. Peter tells us that Noah was a preacher of righteousness (2 Pet. 2:5). Therefore, we can see that Jesus preached through Noah to those wicked people of his day. To help clarify this idea notice what Macknight said:

> For it is certain that our Lord, after his resurrection, did not go personally to the Gentiles to preach peace to them: he preached to them by his apostles only. But if Christ is said by Paul to go and do, what he did by his apostles, he may with equal propriety be said by Peter, to go and do, what he did by his prophet Noah (Macknight 620).

143

We can also see a connection between Jesus' preaching through the Holy Spirit who in turn preached through humans. Jesus said: "However, when He, the Spirit of truth, has come, He will guide you into all truth; for He will not speak on His own *authority,* but whatever He hears He will speak; and He will tell you things to come. "He will glorify Me, for He will take of what is Mine and declare *it* to you" (Jn. 16:13-14). As the inspired apostles spoke by the inspiration of the Holy Spirit, they were in essence allowing Jesus to preach through them (1 Cor. 2:13). The Holy Spirit also caused the prophets of the Old Testament and Noah to proclaim the Word of God (Gen. 6:3; 2 Pet. 1:20-21), which confirms how Jesus could preach through Noah to those wicked people while they were still alive. So, when Peter is talking about the spirits in prison, he is talking about where these wicked people were at the time of his writing, and they will remain in the place of torment until the Day of Judgment.

It was during the time of Noah that the Divine longsuffering waited until the ark was built. It took Noah over 100 years to build the ark, but God patiently waited while he carried out his task. When the ark was completed and the animals were on board, Noah and his family went into the ark, and God shut them in (Gen. 7:16). It rained for forty days and flooded all the earth (Gen. 7:17). Only those eight souls were saved by the water. Some might say the ark saved them and not the water. It is true that the ark was the vessel that kept them from dying in the flood, but it was the water that saved them and transported them away from the sinful world.

While this event deals with their physical salvation, Peter makes a comparison of how baptism saves us spiritually. Noah's salvation is the type, and our salvation through water baptism in the antitype. *Type* is a figure or representative of something to come, and *antitype* is the reality of the type. For instance, if I step in the mud, the impression I leave is the type, but my foot is the antitype because it is the reality of the type. The Old Testament is full of types, and the New Testament is full of antitypes.

For example, Hebrews 10:1 teaches that the Law of Moses was a shadow or representation of what we have under the new covenant. Paul calls Adam a type of Christ (Rom. 5:14), and he compared the difference between Adam and Jesus in his letter to the Corinthians (1 Cor. 15:45-49). In Hebrews 9:24, the writer teaches that the holy place made with hands is the type, but the antitype is heaven itself. More examples could be given, but these should be enough to show that Noah's salvation was the type, but salvation through baptism is the reality or antitype.

Some compare baptism to a wedding ring. They say the wedding ring is symbolic of the couple already being married, and baptism is symbolic of a person already being saved. Based on the evidence we have looked at so far, we can know that baptism saves us and is not symbolic of a person already being saved because it is the reality of salvation. In the chart on the next page, notice how Noah's salvation compares with our salvation.

NOAH'S SALVATION THE TYPE	OUR SALVATION THE ANTITYPE
God offered them salvation	God offers us salvation
Noah had to have faith in God	We have to have faith in God
Noah had the choice to be saved or lost	We have the choice to be saved or lost
Noah was told what he must do to accept God' salvation, which was building the ark	We are told what to do to accept God's salvation, which is believing, confessing, repenting, and being baptized
God was longsuffering while He waited for Noah to build the ark	God is longsuffering for us while He waits for us to obey the gospel (2 Pet. 3:9)
Noah and his family had to complete what God told them to do before He saved them with water	We have to complete what God has told us to do before He will save us at our baptism in water
All those who did not obey God's Word through Noah's preaching perished	All those who do not obey God's Word are lost and they will perish (2 Thes. 1:8)
The element God used to save them from the sinful world was water	The element God uses to save us from the sinful world is water
Only a few were saved	Only a few will be saved (Mt. 7:14)

Obviously, the baptism Peter is talking about is water baptism, and he clearly states that water baptism is what saves us. Those who teach that Holy Spirit baptism is necessary for salvation are forced to say that Peter is talking about Holy Spirit baptism. Of course, this cannot be true because Peter draws the comparison between the water that saved those eight souls and how baptism in water saves us. As I have stated in other chapters, it is not the water itself that saves,

146

but it is the place God has designated that we will be saved by our faith in the working of God (Col. 2:12).

When Peter said that baptism was "not the removal of the filth of the flesh, but the answer of a good conscience toward God," it is clear that he was referring to water baptism. He is explaining, especially to the Jews, that the baptism that saves is not the removal of filth from the body. This fact proves the baptism he was talking about could be perceived as removing filth from the body, which only makes sense if it was being done in water. The reason this was important for the Jews to hear was because they were used to washing themselves before they entered the temple to make themselves physically clean. However, the baptism in water Peter was talking about was for an inward cleaning of the soul. The only way this was made possible was by the death, burial, and resurrection of Jesus. Otherwise, there would no be hope for us, and we would all be lost in our sins (1 Cor. 15:12-19).

When Peter said that baptism is the answer or appeal of a good conscience toward God, some argue that baptism is a response to a good conscience; so we are saved before baptism. If that were true, then anyone who has a good conscience would be saved, yet we know that is not true. Even Saul had a good conscience when he was persecuting Christians, but he was still lost until he had his sins washed away (Acts 22:16; 23:1). Many people can claim they have a good conscience about their lives no matter how sinful they may be, but it does not make them saved. Our conscience can become seared with a hot iron (1 Tim. 4:2) if we do not allow God to direct our footsteps (Jer. 10:23; Pro. 3:5-6). The only way we can have a good conscience that is pleasing to God is by having our sins removed and by living a faithful life to God (2 Cor. 1:12; 1 Tim. 1:5). According to Peter, baptism is an answer or an appeal for a good conscience because it is the time when we receive the forgiveness of our sins (Acts 2:38).

The Greek word for answer or appeal is *eperotema*, and it is only used one time in the New Testament. It has several meanings: inquiry, request, appeal, answer, prayer, craving, integration, pledge, or question.

Thayer notes: "…1 Pet. 3:21: "which (baptism) now saves us (you) not because in receiving it we (ye) have put away the filth of the flesh, but because we (ye) have earnestly sought a conscience reconciled to God…."

BDAG notes: "…an appeal to God for a clear conscience 1 Pt 3:21…."

Kittel notes: "Baptism does not confer physical cleansing but saves as a request for forgiveness …." (262).

All three of these quotes show that a good conscience comes after your baptism. Even if a good conscience preceded baptism, I have already shown that it would not make that person saved. Based on the evidence I have given, it should be clear that salvation does not happen until we are baptized, and we cannot have a good conscience, by God's standards, without it.

Since baptism is an appeal to a good conscience, it also proves that the person being baptized must know what he is doing, which teaches against infant baptism. A baby cannot desire a good conscience concerning his baptism because he has no idea why he is being "baptized."

One thing we need to keep in mind is that being baptized into Jesus for the remission of sins is only the beginning of our salvation, and it is the easiest part. The challenge is remaining faithful until we die. If we do, our eternal salvation will be realized (Rev. 2:10).

There is a false doctrine known as "once saved, always saved." This doctrine would allow me to get saved today and then return to my worldly ways tomorrow, laughing all the way, knowing that I will be saved no matter what I do. This teaching does not make any sense, and it goes against the entire thrust of the Bible. When we examine the Old Testament, the Jews were God's people, but they had a problem with sin. Every time they turned their back on God, they were punished, which shows that God does not tolerate those who live in sin. Sin separates us from God, and it will cause us to be spiritually dead (Rom. 6:23). If "once saved, always saved" is true, then we can live in sin as much as we want and still go to heaven.

To disprove this doctrine, all we have to do is notice a few verses from God's Word:

For if we sin willfully after we have received the knowledge of the truth, there no longer remains a sacrifice for sins, but a certain fearful expectation of judgment, and fiery indignation which will devour the adversaries (Heb. 26-27).

For *it is* impossible for those who were once enlightened, and have tasted the heavenly gift, and have become partakers of the Holy Spirit, and have tasted the good word of God and the powers of the age to come, if they fall away, to renew them again to repentance, since they crucify again for themselves the Son of God, and put *Him* to an open shame (Heb. 6:4).

Whoever transgresses and does not abide in the doctrine of Christ does not have God. He who abides in the doctrine of Christ has both the Father and the Son (2 John 1:9).

149

For if, after they have escaped the pollutions of the world through the knowledge of the Lord and Savior Jesus Christ, they are again entangled in them and overcome, the latter end is worse for them than the beginning (2 Pet. 2:20).

Therefore let him who thinks he stands take heed lest he fall (1 Cor. 10:12).

Therefore we must give the more earnest heed to the things we have heard, lest we drift away (Heb. 2:1).

You have become estranged from Christ, you who attempt to be justified by law; you have fallen from grace (Gal. 5:4).

These verses are just a few out of hundreds of verses that teach that we can fall from our salvation if we do not remain faithful to God by keeping His Word. This truth is the reason Paul describes the life of a Christian as running a race and striving to win the prize (1 Cor. 9:24). Jesus only promises us the crown of life if we remain faithful until the end of our life (Rev. 2:10). As Paul told Timothy, "Fight the good fight of faith, lay hold on eternal life…" (1 Tim. 6:12). Dear reader, I hope you will choose to travel the difficult road that leads to the narrow gate (Mt. 7:14) by walking in the light (1 Jn. 1:7).

One last objection I want to deal with comes from a question that is designed to play on the emotions of others. What if someone believes, repents, and confesses Jesus as Lord, and then on his way to get baptized, he is killed? Wouldn't he be saved without baptism? Before I answer this question, another question needs to be asked. What if an atheist decided he wanted to have a Bible study with a Christian, and as he began to study, he had a heart attack? What if he was going to believe, don't you think he would be saved without belief? Most would answer no because they understand that belief is necessary for salvation, but the same is true with baptism because it is necessary as well. So, we must answer questions like these the same way.

Now let's consider the possibility that God will make an exception for the person that was going to be baptized since he was in the process of obeying what God had commanded him to do. The first question that we need to ask ourselves is how would that exception affect us? Even if we could prove that God will make exceptions under certain circumstances, those exceptions would only apply to a few, and it would not change what God wants us to do under normal circumstances. Even if we allowed for exceptions, which are not taught in the New Testament, if nothing is preventing us from being baptized into Christ for the remission of sins, and we choose not do it, we will be lost.

In conclusion, we have learned that Noah's salvation by water is the type, and our salvation in water baptism in the antitype. Our baptism is not the removal of dirt, but it does wash away our sins (Acts 22:16) by our faith in the working of God (Col. 2:12). Once we are saved, we must continue to be faithful, or we can lose our salvation (Gal. 5:4). No matter how many exceptions people may dream up that might prevent someone from being baptized, these exceptions do not prevent the majority from being baptized.

Questions

1. What is Purgatory?
2. What did Peter mean when he said, "He went and preached to the spirits in prison?"
3. Compare Noah's Salvation to ours.
4. When Peter taught that baptism is an answer of a good conscience toward God, what does that teach us?
5. Can we ever become lost once we are saved?

THREE COMMON ARGUMENTS   12

The three most common arguments people use to teach that baptism is not essential for salvation are *the thief on the cross*, *saved by grace alone*, and *Paul was not sent to baptize*. We will examine each of these arguments, and we will learn that none of them teaches that baptism is not essential for salvation.

Our first argument comes from the cross:

Then one of the criminals who were hanged blasphemed Him, saying, "If You are the Christ, save Yourself and us." But the other, answering, rebuked him, saying, "Do you not even fear God, seeing you are under the same condemnation? "And we indeed justly, for we receive the due reward of our deeds; but this Man has done nothing wrong."   Then he said to Jesus, "Lord, remember me when You come into Your kingdom." And Jesus said to him, "Assuredly, I say to you, today you will be with Me in Paradise (Lk. 23:39-43).

They argue that the thief was saved without baptism; therefore baptism does not save. This argument is the most common one people use, but as we are about to learn, it is one of the weakest arguments a person could use because it does not apply to us today.

Everything we know about these two thieves is recorded in the four Gospels (Mt. 27:38, 44; Mk. 15:27-28, 32; Lk. 23:32-33, 39-43; Jn. 19:18, 32), and Isaiah prophesied about this event (Isa. 53). One thief was on His right, and the other was on His left. Even though they were being crucified, they both mocked Him. However, about halfway through their painful crucifixion, one of the thieves changed his attitude, and he rebuked the other thief for blaspheming Jesus.

There are two possibilities for this man's change of heart. Either he learned about Jesus and what He stood for while hanging on the cross with Him for several hours, or he learned about Jesus before the crucifixion. While it is possible the thief could have learned about Jesus while hanging on the cross, it is unlikely because nothing in the Bible suggests that he was taught anything. It certainly was not the setting for teaching or learning. Notice what the thief understood:

- He believed in God.
- He understood that he and the other thief had sinned, and their punishment was deserved.
- He believed that Jesus was innocent even though most were mocking Him.
- He believed that Jesus was the King and that His death would not be the end of His life. Instead, it would cause Him to come into His kingdom.
- He believed that Jesus could grant His request of remembering him in His kingdom.

Since he had this much knowledge about Jesus, it seems more logical that he had learned about Jesus before the cross.

Those who use the "thief on the cross" argument assume this thief had not been baptized. However, based on the knowledge of this thief, it is possible that he was taught about Jesus and the kingdom to come by either John the Baptist or others. It is also possible that he was baptized with John's baptism because Matthew wrote: "Then Jerusalem, all Judea, and all the region around the Jordan went out to him and were baptized by him in the Jordan, confessing their sins" (Mat 3:5-6). So, it is possible this thief was one of those that had come to John or maybe he was baptized by one of Jesus' disciples (Jn. 4:1-2). However, based on the information we have, we cannot dogmatically say if this thief was or was not baptized. Just as I cannot say for sure that he was baptized, neither can those who use the "thief on the cross" argument prove that he was not baptized.

We also need to consider that each period of Biblical time has its own unique set of laws. For instance, those under the patriarchal period were not required to be baptized or to partake of the Lord's Supper. Those under the Law of Moses had to offer up animal sacrifices and give tithes, but Christians are not required to do this because we are under the Law of Christ (Gal. 6:2; 1 Cor. 9:21).

When Jesus was on the earth, it was a unique period of time. During Jesus' ministry, He had the unique ability and authority to forgive people of their sins. For instance, when the four friends brought the paralyzed man before Jesus, Mark records: "When Jesus saw their faith, He said to the paralytic: 'Son, your sins are forgiven you'" (Mk. 2:5). When Jesus said this, it upset the opposing Jews, but Jesus told them: "Which is easier, to say to the paralytic, '*Your* sins are forgiven you,' or to say, 'Arise, take up your bed and walk'? But that you may know that the Son of Man has power on earth to forgive sins" -- He said to the paralytic, "I say to you, arise, take up your bed, and go to your house." (Mk. 2:9-11). In this instance, the man was healed because of the faith of his four friends. If we are going to claim what Jesus did during His earthly ministry applies today, then we need to teach that our faith can cause Jesus to forgive our friend's sin. If we follow this logic, it means that our friend could be saved without belief, repentance, or confessing Jesus as Lord. We know that salvation cannot be obtained this way because Paul teaches us that we must all stand before the judgment seat of Christ and give an account for what we have done (2 Cor. 5:10).

Another example would be when Jesus forgave the woman's sins who wept on His feet, wiped them off with her hair, kissed them repeatedly, and anointed them with oil (Lk. 7:37-50). Again, this does not apply to us today because we could not do this since Jesus is no longer on the earth. The same thing is true about the thief on the cross. When Jesus said he would be in paradise with Him, He had the authority to do this. Even if the thief had not been baptized, Jesus could have forgiven him of his sins. Since this was a unique time that only happened while Jesus was alive on the earth, the thief on the cross cannot be used by anybody today to prove that baptism is not part of the salvation plan.

Additionally, the only baptism the thief could have received was the baptism John preached because the baptism Jesus commanded did not go into effect until after the cross when He gave The Great Commission (Mt. 28:19; Mk. 16:16). Before this new baptism came into to effect, Jesus had to die.

For where there *is* a testament, there must also of necessity be the death of the testator. For a testament *is* in force after men are dead, since it has no power at all while the testator lives (Heb. 9:16-17).

We can relate to this today because a person's will does not go into effect until he dies, and then it must be probated. While the thief died shortly after Jesus, he was not alive to hear the New Testament probated, which is why "the thief on the cross" argument is so weak. The thief on the cross died before The Great Commission was commanded, so he could not have been baptized into Christ for the remission of sins even if he wanted to. So, the thief on the cross cannot serve as an example for the Christian today because we are under the new covenant, which states that we must be baptized in the name of Jesus for the remission of our sins (Acts 2:38).

Our second argument comes from what Paul wrote to the Ephesians:

For by grace you have been saved through faith, and that not of yourselves; *it is* **the gift of God, not of works, lest anyone should boast (Eph. 2:8-9).**

This is another favorite text of those who teach against the necessity of baptism. They teach that Paul was saying that we are saved by grace through "faith alone" without any works. Therefore, baptism cannot be necessary because it is a work of man.

On the surface, this argument may sound like a strong one for the "faith only" doctrine, but as we will learn, this argument is based on a faulty interpretation of the Scriptures. To help us understand what Paul is talking about, we need to examine the context and background.

On Paul's third mission journey, he made his way into Ephesus where he found twelve men that were baptized with John's baptism (Acts 19). When he learned they had not received the Holy Spirit, he taught them that they must be baptized in the name of Jesus, and they obeyed and were baptized. Paul stayed about three years at Ephesus, teaching and preaching about Jesus. Later, when Paul was in prison at Rome, he wrote this letter to the Christians at Ephesus, which could have included those twelve men that he baptized in the name of Jesus. When Paul reminded these Christians that they were saved by grace through faith, he was including baptism in this statement, which is proven further by looking at the context.

In Ephesians 1:19-23, we learn that God raised Jesus from the dead, and in Ephesians 2, we learn how God made us alive with Christ. Notice the first seven verses:

And you *He made alive,* who were dead in trespasses and sins, in which you once walked according to the course of this world, according to the prince of the power of the air, the spirit who now works in the sons of disobedience, among whom also we all once conducted ourselves in the lusts of our flesh, fulfilling the desires of the flesh and of the mind, and were by nature children of wrath, just as the others. But God, who is rich in mercy, because of His great love with which He loved us, even when we were dead in trespasses, made us alive together with Christ (by grace you have been saved), and raised *us* up together, and made *us* sit together in the heavenly *places* in Christ Jesus, that in the ages to come He might show the exceeding riches of His grace in *His* kindness toward us in Christ Jesus (Eph. 2:1-7).

Paul reminded them that they were lost in their sins because they had lived according to the world, but God loved them enough to allow them to be made alive with Jesus. These sinful people did not deserve or earn their salvation, but God made their salvation possible by His grace through the blood of Jesus (Eph. 2:13). The question becomes, when were these sinners at Ephesus made alive with Christ? This is an important question to answer because whatever is associated with them being made alive with Christ will be included in the statement: "By grace you have been saved."

To answer this question, all we have to do is examine more of Paul's writings. The first place we want to look is his letter to the Colossians. This letter was written from the prison at Rome, and it is considered to be similar to the letter to the Ephesians. When we compare the two letters, we will discover that they make the same points about salvation.

However, Colossians does not mention grace, but it does mention baptism, and Ephesians does not mention baptism, but it does mention grace. In the Gospels, we have to read all four accounts to get the complete picture of an event. This same method must also be done with what Paul wrote about salvation, especially in these two similar accounts. Notice what he said in his letter to the Colossians:

In Him you were also circumcised with the circumcision made without hands, by putting off the body of the sins of the flesh, by the circumcision of Christ, buried with Him in baptism, in which you also were raised with *Him* through faith in the working of God, who raised Him from the dead. And you, being dead in your trespasses and the uncircumcision of your flesh, He has made alive together with Him, having forgiven you all trespasses (Col. 2:11-13).

Paul is teaching us that these sinners were made alive with Jesus when they were baptized. They knew this was happening at their baptism because of their faith in the working of God. This passage proves that being saved by grace includes being baptized into Christ. Remember their argument states that baptism is a work of man, but Paul said it was a work of God, which can also be seen in what Paul wrote to Titus:

But when the kindness and the love of God our Savior toward man appeared, not by works of righteousness which we have done, but according to His mercy He saved us, through the washing of regeneration and renewing of the Holy Spirit whom He poured out on us abundantly through Jesus Christ our Savior, that having been justified by His grace we should become heirs according to the hope of eternal life (Tit. 3:4-7).

We are not saved by works of righteousness that we have done, which is referring to works of merit. Instead, we are

159

saved by God through the washing of regeneration and re-newing of the Holy Spirit. By this we have been justified by grace. Paul is teaching the same thing as he did in Ephesians 2. Washing of regeneration is a reference to baptism, and even the majority of denominational scholars that teach against the necessity of baptism agree that this is referring to water baptism. For instance, John Calvin, A.T. Robertson, John Wesley, Adam Clark, Albert Barnes, Alvah Hovey, and J.E. Huther all agree this is talking about baptism. So, this verse proves once again that baptism is a work of God that saves us and causes us to be justified by His grace.

The renewing of the Holy Spirit refers to the work of the Holy Spirit through the Word of God, which saves (Jam. 1:21). Peter said: "Since you have purified your souls in obey-ing the truth through the Spirit in sincere love of the breth-ren, love one another fervently with a pure heart, having been born again, not of corruptible seed but incorruptible, through the word of God which lives and abides forever" (1 Pet. 1:22-23). This passage agrees with what Jesus said to Nicodemus: "Most assuredly, I say to you, unless one is born of water and the Spirit, he cannot enter the kingdom of God" (Jn.3:5). These verses prove that the Holy Spirit works through the Word, and we must obey that Word if we want to have salva-tion.

Paul also teaches in Colossians 2:11-13 that our sins are for-given at the point of baptism. The comparison between these two letters is enough to prove that baptism is necessary for salvation, but I want to drive the point home. In Paul's letter to the Romans, he used the same language to prove that bap-tism is the point at which a person dies with Christ and is made alive with Him.

Or do you not know that as many of us as were baptized into Christ Jesus were baptized into His death? Therefore we were buried with Him through baptism

160

into death, that just as Christ was raised from the dead by the glory of the Father, even so we also should walk in newness of life. For if we have been united together in the likeness of His death, certainly we also shall be *in the likeness* of *His* resurrection, knowing this, that our old man was crucified with *Him,* that the body of sin might be done away with, that we should no longer be slaves of sin. For he who has died has been freed from sin. Now if we died with Christ, we believe that we shall also live with Him, knowing that Christ, having been raised from the dead, dies no more. Death no longer has dominion over Him. For *the death* that He died, He died to sin once for all; but *the life* that He lives, He lives to God. Likewise you also, reckon yourselves to be dead indeed to sin, but alive to God in Christ Jesus our Lord (Rom. 6:3-11).

Just as God was involved is raising Jesus from the dead, He is going to be involved in what takes place at our baptism. At the point of baptism, we die with Jesus, we are united with Him, and we are made alive with Him. Again, Paul teaches that our sins are removed at the point of baptism. Notice what else Paul said:

For you are all sons of God through faith in Christ Jesus. For as many of you as were baptized into Christ have put on Christ (Gal. 3:26-27).

They were sons of God through faith, but this faith was not mere belief because it included baptism. Without baptism they could not be put into Christ. All the verses we have examined show that God has given us salvation through grace, but we have to accept that grace by having an obedient faith to the Word of God, which is what is meant by: "For by grace you have been saved through faith, and that not of yourselves; *it is* the gift of God, not of works, lest anyone should boast" (Eph. 2:8-9).

We need to understand that salvation is the gift of God (Rom. 6:23), and when we accept God's salvation by believing, repenting, confessing Jesus as Lord, and being baptized, we have not earned or merited our salvation. When we remain faithful and do good works to the end of our life, we still have not earned or merited our salvation. Instead, we are simply doing what God has asked us to do (Lk.17:7-10), and we have no reason to boast in these things because salvation is only possible through God.

When Paul said that our salvation is not of works, he was talking about works of merit and not works of obedience. If he meant works in general, then belief would be excluded from salvation because Jesus' disciples wanted to know how they might work the works of God. Jesus told them: "This is the work of God, that you believe in Him whom He sent" (Jn. 6:29). Believing in Jesus is called a work, yet believing is Jesus is necessary for salvation (Jn. 3:36; 8:24). I have already shown from Colossians 2:12 that baptism is a work of God. Just like belief, baptism is a work of obedience that is necessary for salvation as Peter said: "There is also an antitype which now saves us – baptism..." (1 Pet. 3:21).

If works of obedience are not necessary for salvation, then why did Paul write the following to the Philippians: "Therefore, my beloved, as you have always obeyed, not as in my presence only, but now much more in my absence, work out your own salvation with fear and trembling" (2:12)? Why did the writer of Hebrews say that Jesus was the "author of eternal salvation to all who obey Him" (5:9)? Why did James write: "You see then that a man is justified by works, and not by faith only" (2:24)? Why did Paul teach that God would take vengeance "on those who do not know God, and on those who do not obey the gospel of our Lord Jesus Christ" (2 Thes. 1:8)?

All these verses would not make sense if works in general were excluded. This fact proves there are two different kinds of works. There are works of merit, which will not save a person, and works of obedience, which are necessary in accepting God's grace. We can see this again as Paul continues his letter to the Ephesians:

For we are His workmanship, created in Christ Jesus for good works, which God prepared beforehand that we should walk in them (Eph. 2:10).

While we cannot merit our salvation with works, Paul tells us to walk in good works. Since the grace of God teaches us to have obedient works Paul said: "For the grace of God that brings salvation has appeared to all men, teaching us that, denying ungodliness and worldly lusts, we should live soberly, righteously, and godly in the present age" (Titus 2:11-12). All these things that grace teaches us to do are works of obedience.

Those who claim that we are saved by grace alone would have to admit that all are saved no matter who they are because Paul said that grace has appeared to all men. If this argument is true, then people like Adolf Hitler and Saddam Hussein are saved if we are saved by grace alone. Those who teach that grace alone or faith alone saves cannot show one Scripture that makes this statement. In fact, the only time the word *faith* and *only* appear in the Bible is when James said we are not justified by faith only (Jam. 2:24).

God has always demanded an obedient faith to accept His grace in the Old Testament and the New Testament. While many examples could be given, I want to illustrate this fact by the following chart:

NOAH'S SALVATION AND OURS

Noah's Salvation	Our Salvation
Grace (Gen. 6:8)	Grace (Eph. 2:8)
Obedient Faith (Heb. 11:7; Gen. 6:22)	Obedient Faith (Heb. 5: 8-9; Jn. 14:15)
Water (1 Pet. 3:20)	Water (1 Pet. 3:21)

Noah found grace in the sight of God, and He offered him and his family salvation. However, they had to accept this gift of grace by building the ark, which took an obedient faith. God did not bring about their salvation until they completed the ark and entered it. He flooded the world with water and killed all the humans that were left, but Noah and his family was saved from the wicked world by the water because it transported them away from the sinful world.

In a similar way, God offers us His grace, but we must have an obedient faith to receive it. We will not receive the forgiveness of sins until we have done what has been asked of us. After we have believed, repented, and confessed Jesus as Lord, we must then be baptized in water before we are saved and our sins are forgiven. This principle could also be illustrated with Moses and the children of Israel, Joshua and the walls of Jericho, and Naaman the leper.

All these examples and Scriptures prove that grace is God's part, and an obedient faith is our part. So, we are not saved by grace or faith alone. Instead, we are saved by God's grace by accepting it through an obedient faith, and by keeping an obedient faith for the rest of our lives because it is possible for us to fall from grace (Gal. 5:4).

Before we leave this topic, I want to deal with an argument some Calvinists use on Ephesians 2:8. Since they believe some are predestined to be saved and others are predestined to be lost, they teach that the gift of God in Ephesians 2:8 is faith. In other words, a person has no choice if he is going to be saved or not because God will cause him to have faith or he will not have it. Of course this view would have God showing partiality, which He does not do (Acts 10:34-35).

To prove that it is not grammatically possible for the gift of God to be faith in Ephesians 2:8, notice what Wayne Jackson wrote:

> The passage cited above (Eph. 2:8), as a proof-text for the idea that "faith" is strictly a "gift," does not, in fact, teach that idea at all. The text reads as follows:
>
> "...for by grace have you been saved through faith; and that not of your selves, it is the gift of God...."
>
> There is no specifically-stated antecedent for "gift" in this context. However, it is to be inferred. The gift is the salvation that is implied by the verb "saved."
>
> "For by grace are you saved through faith; and this not of yourselves, it [the salvation] is the gift of God."
>
> Grammatically speaking, there is no agreement between "faith" and "gift." Faith (pisteos) in the Greek Testament is a feminine form, while "gift" (doron) is neuter gender. The "gift" is not "faith" (*Is Faith the Gift Ephesians 2:8?* christiancourier.com).

Also in his article Mr. Jackson noted:

> Even John Calvin interpreted the "gift" of this passage as "salvation," and not faith (The Epistle to the Ephesians, Edinburgh: Oliver & Boyd, 1965, p. 144). This is in perfect harmony with Paul's declaration elsewhere that the "gift of God is eternal life" (Rom. 6:23).

Not even John Calvin was willing to go against the grammar of this text, even though some of his followers are, which should be enough proof that the gift of God is salvation and not faith. However, it is true that faith comes from God, but Paul explains: "So then faith *comes* by hearing, and hearing by the word of God" (Rom. 10:17). So, we can all have faith if we are willing to accept and obey what we hear from the Word of God. It is God's desire that we will be saved and come to the knowledge of the truth (1 Tim. 2:4).

Our third argument comes from Paul's writing to the Corinthians:

Now I plead with you, brethren, by the name of our Lord Jesus Christ, that you all speak the same thing, and *that* there be no divisions among you, but *that* you be perfectly joined together in the same mind and in the same judgment. For it has been declared to me concerning you, my brethren, by those of Chloe's *household,* that there are contentions among you. Now I say this, that each of you says, "I am of Paul," or "I am of Apollos," or "I am of Cephas," or "I am of Christ." Is Christ divided? Was Paul crucified for you? Or were you baptized in the name of Paul? I thank God that I baptized none of you except Crispus and Gaius, lest anyone should say that I had baptized in my own name. Yes, I also baptized the household of Stephanas. Besides, I do not know whether I baptized any other.

For Christ did not send me to baptize, but to preach the gospel, not with wisdom of words, lest the cross of Christ should be made of no effect (1 Cor. 1:10-17).

Their argument is based on verse 17. When Paul said: "For Christ did not send me to baptize, but to preach the gospel," they say Paul was teaching that baptism is not part of the gospel. Therefore, it is not essential for our salvation because the gospel saves (Rom. 1:16), which is the reason he was sent to preach and not sent to baptize. Those who oppose the necessity of baptism think this argument is a strong one, but as we will learn, it is not.

The first thing that we need to realize when we interpret the meaning of a Scripture is that it cannot contradict other clear passages on this topic. This fact proves that their argument is false because it would cause Paul to contradict other plain Scriptures that prove that baptism is part of the gospel and is essential for our salvation.

When Jesus gave The Great Commission, He told His disciples: "He who believes and is baptized will be saved ..." (Mk. 16:16), and they were commanded to baptize "them in the name of the Father and of the Son and of the Holy Spirit" (Mt. 28:19). These verses teach that baptism is part of the gospel. When the apostles were asked: "Men *and* brethren, what shall we do?" (Acts 2:37), Peter told them: "Repent, and let every one of you be baptized in the name of Jesus Christ for the remission of sins..." (Acts 2:38). When Philip preached Jesus to the Ethiopian eunuch, he understood that baptism was part of the gospel because he said: "See, *here is* water. What hinders me from being baptized?" (Acts 8:36). These examples are enough to prove that baptism is part of the gospel and essential for salvation.

Since Paul is being accused of saying that baptism is not essential, let us examine what Paul said about baptism. The first thing I want to point out is that Paul teaches more about baptism then anyone else in the Bible. When Paul was converted to Christianity, he was baptized for the remission of his sins (Acts 22:16). When he went around preaching the gospel, people were baptized including many Corinthians (Acts 18:8). Lydia, her household, and the Philippian jailer's family were baptized because they heard the gospel from Paul (Acts 16:14-15; 27-34). He also baptized some men who had been baptized with John's baptism (Acts 19:1-5). Even in our main text, Paul mentioned that he baptized Crispus, Gaius, and the household of Stephanas (1 Cor. 1:14-16). Does it make sense that Paul would talk about baptizing some and then say in the next verse that he was not sent to baptize because it was not part of the gospel? Absolutely not! Instead, these examples show that baptism was part of the gospel and that Paul administered baptism occasionally.

To take this a step further, Paul taught that baptism:
- Puts a person into the body of Christ (1 Cor. 12:13).
- Puts a person into Christ (Rom 6:3; Gal. 3:27).
- Is when a person is buried with Christ (Rom. 6:4; Col. 2:12).
- Is when a person is united with Christ (Rom. 6:5).
- Is when a person's sins are forgiven (Rom. 6:7; Col. 2:13; Acts 22:16).

Other examples and Scriptures could be given, but these are enough to show that Paul was not saying that baptism was not part of the gospel, nor was he saying that baptism was not essential for our salvation. If we are going to rightly divide the Word of God, then we must interpret what Paul said based on all the evidence we have looked at so far.

The first thing that we need to do is examine the context so we can know why Paul said what he did. Paul was writing this letter to the church at Corinth, and he was addressing a unity problem. Some of these Christians were dividing themselves into different groups and calling themselves after the men that taught them, but Paul asked them: "Is Christ divided? Was Paul crucified for you? Or were you baptized in the name of Paul?" (1 Cor. 1:13).

In this context, Paul is condemning division in the body of Christ and Christians calling themselves after men. Yet, that is exactly what denominationalism is all about. Let the reader understand that Paul is condemning denominations in this text.

The questions Paul asked also show the necessity of baptism. He taught that it takes two things to belong to Paul, Apollos, Cephas, or Christ. First, the person had to be crucified for you. Second, you had to be baptized in the name of that person. To be baptized in the name of Paul would make you belong to Paul, but Paul was not crucified for you. However, Jesus was. So, if a person wants to belong to Jesus, he has to be baptized in the name of Jesus, which is the only way that a person can say, "I am of Christ." As Paul wrote to the Galatians: "For as many of you as were baptized into Christ have put on Christ" (Gal. 3:27). As I showed in the chapter on The Great Commission, baptism puts a person into the possession and protection of the Godhead, which agrees with what Paul was teaching.

Next, Paul said: "I thank God that I baptized none of you except Crispus and Gaius, lest anyone should say that I had baptized in my own name. Yes, I also baptized the household of Stephanas. Besides, I do not know whether I baptized any other." Paul was thankful he had not baptized all these people because he did not want them to be confused and think he had baptized them in his own name. Some of these men were even calling themselves after Paul just because he had taught them the gospel. Just imagine how much stronger their conviction would be if Paul had baptized them as well.

To understand the reason they were doing this, we have to put ourselves in their shoes. When Paul would preach the gospel in a new area, he would prove the words he was speaking was from God by doing miracles and signs (Mk. 16:20). When these first century people heard the words and saw the signs, they would tend to make Paul into a God in their eyes like they did at Lystra (Acts 14:11). This behavior is the reason Paul was glad that he had not baptized most of these people.

Finally, Paul said: "For Christ did not send me to baptize, but to preach the gospel, not with wisdom of words, lest the cross of Christ should be made of no effect." Since we have examined the whole counsel of God, we can know that Paul was not saying that baptism is not part of the gospel, and he was not saying that baptism was not part of his ministry as an apostle. If Jesus did not send Paul to baptize, then he disobeyed Him several times in his ministry including the names he just mentioned that he baptized. It would also make Jesus exclude Paul from the command of The Great Commission: "Go therefore and make disciples of all the nations, baptizing them in the name of the Father and of the Son and of the Holy Spirit…" (Mt. 28:19).

Based on the evidence I have given, if we are honest with ourselves, we can see that Paul was not excluding baptism from salvation. Instead, he was saying that his main role as an apostle was to preach the gospel and not to baptize because any Christian could baptize another. Besides, we have already learned there were times when Paul did baptize.

The reason it does not matter if an apostle, elder, preacher, or another Christian baptizes a person is that the person that is dipping the unsaved person under the water is just aiding him in his baptism. What takes place in the baptism has nothing to do with the person that is aiding them because God is the one that is doing the work. As Paul said: "In Him you were also circumcised with the circumcision made without hands, by putting off the body of the sins of the flesh, by the circumcision of Christ, buried with Him in baptism, in which you also were raised with *Him* through faith in the working of God, who raised Him from the dead" (Col. 2:11-12). So, Paul was not saying that he was not sent to baptize at all, but that he was not sent to baptize only because any Christian could have baptized the unsaved after Paul had taught them the gospel.

In conclusion, we have learned that the thief on the cross is a great example of God's forgiveness, but his situation has nothing to do with us because he lived and died at a unique time before the new covenant was probated. We have learned that we are not saved by grace or faith alone, but that we accept God's saving grace by having an obedient faith, which includes being baptized. Finally, we learned that Paul was not excluding baptism from the gospel, he was just saying that his primary mission was to preach the gospel because any Christian could administer it.

Questions

1. What are two possible reasons one of the thieves changed his attitude?
2. Could the thief be baptized with the baptism commanded by Jesus in The Great Commission?
3. Are we saved by grace alone?
4. When are we made alive with Christ?
5. Can we be saved by works of merit?
6. What is the difference between works of merit and works of obedience?
7. Explain why the gift of God is not faith in Ephesians 2:8.
8. What are some of things Paul taught about baptism?
9. Discus why Paul said, "For Christ did not send me to baptize, but to preach the gospel?"

The New Testament was written in Koine Greek, which was the common language of the first century. While the Word of God gives us the perfect definition of *baptism* and how it is to be done, we can learn more about this word by examining how other documents around that era used it. This information is found in various Lexicons in which Greek and Hebrew scholars have studied the Greek and Hebrew of other documents to give us a better idea of the meaning of words such as *baptism*. We need to keep in mind that these Lexicons are not infallible, and sometimes they will offer their own biased opinions. For instance, BDAG says: "Baptism by pouring is allowed in cases of necessity." They suggest that pouring was sometimes used to baptize in certain situations. However, when we study the Scriptures, we will not find an example of pouring associated with baptism; so pouring under certain circumstances is a human invention. Besides, pouring has its own specific Greek words (*ballo, epicheo*), and they are never used to describe a person being baptized into Christ. Also, none of these Lexicons mention sprinkling as being associated with baptism, which has its own Greek word as well (*rhantizo*).

It is also important to understand that the translators of the Bible do not always translate a Greek word into its equivalent English word. Instead, they will transliterate it, which has been done with our word baptism. They took the Greek word *baptisma* and converted the Greek letters to the equivalent English letters and then dropped the last *a*. This transliteration gave us our new English word, *baptism*, which nearly every Bible translation uses. However, if our Greek word *baptisma* had been translated, it would have been rendered as immersion because that is what it means.

The reason it is important that we do a word study on baptism is that we cannot rely on the definition given for *baptism* in the English language. Some dictionaries state that sprinkling, pouring, or immersion are possible definitions for the word *baptism*, which does not agree with the original meaning from the Greek. So, why did we end up with a transliteration of *baptisma* instead of a translation? Edward Wharton offers the following explanation:

> How did we end up with a transliteration instead of a translation? It happened in England during the reign of King James, the son Mary, Queen of Scots. In A.D. 1604, during a conference of the clergy and bishops of the Church of England, King James ordered the Scriptures to be translated into the English language. Forty-seven (47) men of special learning were chosen from church-men, Puritans and scholars having no theological bias. In A.D. 1611, these men produced what is called the "King James Version" of the Bible. In that version there appeared, for the first time, a new English word - "BAPTISM."
>
> This new word came into being because these forty-seven (47) scholars faced a problem. In the Koine Greek manuscripts was this word BAPTISMA which meant "TO IMMERSE."

But, King James was a member of the Church of England and this Anglican church did not immerse. Because of the Catholic apostasy, inherited by the Church of England when they broke with Catholicism in 1534, King James had never been IMMERSED in baptism - he had only been SPRINKLED.

These scholars would not sacrifice their scholastic integrity by saying the word "BAPTISMA" meant "SPRINKLE." That would make them the laughing stock of the world, they TRANSLITERATED the word by putting, in the text of the King James Bible, the English equivalent of the Greek alphabet.

Instead of the text reading: "...arise and be IMMERSED..." they wrote "...arize and be BAPTIZED..." And they did that in every place where the word or a form of the word, BAPTIZE, appeared in the original manuscripts. That is how we got our English word BAPTIZE and BAPTISM (84).

From that point forward, nearly every translation has continued to use the transliterated word *baptism*, which is unfortunate because all it does is add to the confusion of what baptism is all about.

There are two basic meanings of *baptism*.

First, it means to dip, plunge, immerse, or submerge someone or something. This is the way *baptism* is used most of the time in Scripture, and it is the only way it is used to refer to those who were being baptized into Christ for the remission of their sins. There was several different types of baptisms, but when Paul wrote to the Ephesians, there was only one baptism that saved (Eph. 4:4-5), which was the same baptism commanded by Jesus (Mt. 28:19; Mk. 16:16). We can know that one baptism consisted of water (Jn. 3:3-5; Acts 8:38; 10:47-48; 1 Pet. 3:20-21), and a person was fully immersed or buried in the water (Rom. 6:4; Col. 2:12).

Second, it was used to show how someone can be overwhelmed in something. For example, Jesus referred to the suffering He would face at His death as a baptism (Mt. 20:22), and John used the term *baptism with fire*, which describes the eternal punishment that all unbelievers will suffer on the Day of Judgment (Lk. 3:16-17). To provide a more in-depth study of the Greek word *baptizo*, I have provided the following excerpts from several well respected Lexicons:

Friberg Lexicon

4491 βαπτζω fut. **βαπτίσω**; 1aor. **ἐβάπτισα**, mid. **ἐβαπτισάμην**; pf. pass. ptc. **βεβαπτισμένος**; 1aor. pass. **ἐβαπτίσθην**; 1fut. pass. **βαπτισθήσομαι**; strictly *dip, immerse* in water; middle *dip oneself, wash*; in the NT predominately of the use of water in a religious and symbolic sense; (1) of Jewish ritual washings *wash, cleanse, purify by washing* (MK 7.4); (2) as a symbolic rite indicating an aspect of relation to Christ; (a) of John the Baptist's preparatory baptizing with water *baptize* (MT 3.6); (b) of Jesus' transitional baptizing with water (JN 3.22); (c) of Christian baptism with water, identifying a believer with the death of Christ (AC 2.41; RO 6.3); (3) figuratively, in reference to ideas associated with baptism, as an act of commitment and identification; with Moses (1C 10.2); of receiving the Holy Spirit (MT 3.11b); of trial and martyrdom (LU 12.50)

BDAG Lexicon

1400 βαπτίζω

• **βαπτίζω** ...In Gk. lit. gener. to put or go under water in a variety of senses, also fig., e.g. 'soak' Pla., Symp. 176b in wine) in our lit. only in ritual or ceremonial sense ...

1. wash ceremonially for purpose of purification, *wash, purify,* of a broad range of repeated ritual washing rooted in Israelite tradition (cp. Just., D. 46, 2) **Mk 7:4; Lk 11:38;** ... The Law of Purification in Mk 7:1-23 ...

2. to use water in a rite for purpose of renewing or establishing a relationship w. God, *plunge, dip, wash, baptize.* The transliteration 'baptize' signifies the ceremonial character that NT narratives accord such cleansing, but the need of qualifying statements or contextual coloring in the documents indicates that the term β. was not nearly so technical as the transliteration suggests.

a. of dedicatory cleansing associated w. the ministry of John the Baptist (Orig., C. Cels. 1, 47, 4), abs. **J 1:25, 28; 3:23a; 10:40;** hence John is called ὁ βαπτίζων **Mk 1:4; 6:14, 24** ... Pass. **Mt 3:16;** ISm 1:1; oft. *have oneself baptized, get baptized* **Mt 3:13f; Lk 3:7, 12, 21; 7:30; J 3:23b;** ... *w. water* **Mk 1:8a; Lk 3:16a; Ac 1:5a; 11:16a;** ... W. the external element and purpose given ἐν ὕδατι εἰς μετάνοιαν **Mt 3:11a** (AOliver, Is β. used w. ἐν and the Instrumental?: RevExp 35, '38, 190-97).—βαπτίζεσθαι τὸ βάπτισμα Ἰωάννου *undergo John's baptism* **Lk 7:29.** εἰς τί ἐβαπτίσθητε; **Ac 19:3** means, as the answer shows, *in reference to what (baptism) were you baptized?* i.e. what kind of baptism did you receive (as the context indicates, John's baptism was designed to implement repentance as a necessary stage for the reception of Jesus; with the arrival of Jesus the next stage was the receipt of the Holy Spirit in connection with apostolic baptism in the name of Jesus, who was no longer the 'coming one', but the arrived 'Lord')? β. βάπτισμα μετανοίας *administer a repentance baptism* vs. **4;** GEb 13, 74.—S. the lit. on Ἰωάν(ν)ης 1, and on the baptism of Jesus by John …

b. of cleansing performed by Jesus **J 3:22, 26; 4:1;** difft. **4:2** with disclaimer of baptismal activity by Jesus personally.

c. of the Christian sacrament of initiation after Jesus' death (freq. pass.; s. above 2a; Iren. 3, 12, 9 [Harv. II 63, 3]) **Mk 16:16; Ac 2:41; 8:12f, 36, 38; 9:18; 10:47; 16:15, 33; 18:8; 22:16; 1 Cor 1:14-17;** D 7 (where baptism by pouring is allowed in cases of necessity); ISm 8:2.—β. τινὰ εἰς (τὸ) ὄνομά τινος (s. ὄνομα 1dγb) *baptize in* or w. respect to the name of someone: (τοῦ) κυρίου **Ac 8:16; 19:5;** D 9:5; Hv 3, 7, 3. Cp. **1 Cor 1:13, 15.** εἰς τ. ὄν. τ. πατρὸς καὶ τ. υἱοῦ καὶ τ. ἁγίου πνεύματος **Mt 28:19** … **Ac 2:38** text; more briefly εἰς Χριστόν **Gal 3:27; Ro 6:3a.** To be baptized εἰς Χρ. is for Paul an involvement in Christ's death and its implications for the believer … The effect of baptism is to bring all those baptized εἰς ἓν σῶμα **1 Cor 12:13** (perh. wordplay: 'plunged into one body').—W. the purpose given εἰς ἄφεσιν τ. ἁμαρτιῶν **Ac 2:38** … many believe that by being received into the mysteries by the rites (τελεταί) they become more devout, more just, and better in every way.—ὑπὲρ τ. νεκρῶν **1 Cor 15:29a,** s. also vs. **29b,** is obscure because of our limited knowledge of a practice that was evidently obvious to the recipients of Paul's letter; it has been interpr. (1) *in place of the dead,* i.e. vicariously; (2) *for the benefit of the dead,* in var. senses; (3) locally, *over* (the graves of) *the dead;* (4) *on account of the dead,* infl. by their good ex.; of these the last two are the least probable… On the substitution of a ceremony by another person cp. Diod. S. 4, 24, 5: the boys who do not perform the customary sacrifices lose their voices and become as dead persons in the sacred precinct. When someone takes a vow to make the sacrifice for them, their trouble disappears at once.

3. to cause someone to have an extraordinary experience akin to an initiatory water-rite, *to plunge, baptize.* Cp. 'take the plunge' and s. OED 'Plunge' II 5 esp. for the rendering of usage 3c, below.

a. typologically of Israel's passage through the Red Sea εἰς τὸν Μωϋσῆν ἐβαπτίσαντο *they got themselves plunged/ baptized for Moses,* thereby affirming his leadership **1 Cor 10:2 v.l.** (if the pass. ἐβαπτίσθησαν is to be read with N. the point remains the same; but the mid. form puts the onus, as indicated by the context, on the Israelites).

b. of the Holy Spirit (fire) β. τινὰ (ἐν) πνεύματι ἁγίῳ **Mk 1:8** (v.l. + ἐν); **J 1:33; Ac 1:5b; 11:16b;** cp. **1 Cor 12:13** (cp. Just., D. 29, 1). ἐν πν. ἁγ. καὶ πυρί **Mt 3:11b; Lk 3:16b** (JDunn, NovT 14, '72, 81-92). On the oxymoron of baptism w. fire: REisler, Orphisch-dionysische Mysterienged. in d. christl. Antike: Vortr. d. Bibl. Warburg II/2, 1925, 139ff; CEdsman, Le baptême de feu (ASNU 9) '40. JATRobinson, The Baptism of John and Qumran, HTR 50, '57, 175-91; cp. 1QS 4:20f.

c. of martyrdom ... 'overwhelmed by debts' ... 'he drowned the city in misery' ...; **Mk 10:38** (perh. the stark metaph. of impending personal disaster is to be rendered, 'are you prepared to be drowned the way I'm going to be drowned?'); cp. vs. **39; Mt 20:22 v.l.;** in striking contrast to fire **Lk 12:50** ...

179

Thayer's Lexicon

948 βαπτίζω

βαπτίζω; (imperfect ἐβαπτιζον); future βαπτίσω; 1 aorist ἐβάπτισα; passive (present βαπτίζομαι); imperfect ἐβαπτιζομην; perfect participle βεβαπτισμενος; 1 aorist ἐβαπτίσθην; 1 future βαπτισθήσομαι; 1 aorist middle ἐβαπτισαμην; (frequent. (?) from βάπτω, like βαλλίζω from βάλλω); here and there in Plato, Polybius, Diodorus, Strabo, Josephus, Plutarch, others.

I.

1. properly, *to dip repeatedly, to immerse, submerge* (of vessels sunk, Polybius 1, 51, 6; 8, 8, 4; of animals, Diodorus 1, 36).

2. *to cleanse by dipping or submerging, to wash, to make clean with water*; in the middle and the 1 aorist passive *to wash oneself, bathe*; so Mark 7:4 (where WH text ῥαντισωνται); Luke 11:38 (2 Kings 5:14 ἐβαπτίσατο ἐν τῷ Ιορδάνῃ, for טָבַל; Sir. 31:30 (Sir. 34:30; Judith 12:7).

3. metaphorically, *to overwhelm*, as ἰδιωτας ταῖς ἐισφοραις, Diodorus 1, 73; ὀφλημασι, Plutarch, Galba 21; τῇ συμφορά βεβαπτισμενος, Heliodorus Aeth. 2, 3; and alone, to inflict great and abounding calamities on one: ἐβαπτισαν τήν πόλιν, Josephus, b. j. 4, 3, 3; ἡ ἀνομία με βαπτίζει, Isa. 21:4 the Septuagint hence, βαπτίζεσθαι βάπτισμα (cf. Winer's Grammar, 225 (211); (Buttmann, 148 (129)); cf. λούεσθαι τό λουτρόν, Aelian de nat. an. 3, 42), *to be overwhelmed with calamities,* of those who must bear them, Matt. 20:22f Rec.; Mark 10:38 f; Luke 12:50 (cf. the German *etwas auszubaden haben,* and the use of the word e. g. respecting those who cross a river with difficulty, ἕως τῶν μαστῶν οἱ πεζοί βαπτιζόμενοι διέβαινον, Polybius 3,

180

72, 4; (for examples see Sophocles' Lexicon under the word; also T. J. Conant, βαπτίζειν, its meaning and use, N. Y. 1864 (printed also as an Appendix to their revised version of the Gospel of Matthew by the *American Bible Union*); and especially four works by J. W. Dale entitled Classic, Judaic, Johannic, Christic, Baptism, Phil. 1867ff; D. B. Ford, Studies on the Bapt. Quest. (including a review of Dr. Dale's works), Bost. 1879)).

II. In the N. T. it is used particularly of the rite of sacred ablution, first instituted by John the Baptist, afterward by Christ's command received by Christians and adjusted to the contents and nature of their religion (see βάπτισμα, 3), viz., an immersion in water, performed as a sign of the removal of sin, and administered to those who, impelled by a desire for salvation, sought admission to the benefits of the Messiah's kingdom; (for patristic references respecting the mode, ministrant, subjects, etc. of the rite, cf. Sophocles' Lexicon, under the word; Dict. of Chris. Antiq. under the word Baptism). a. The word is used absolutely, *to administer the rite of ablution, to baptize* (Vulgate *baptizo*; Tertullian *tingo, tinguo* (cf. *metgiro*, de corona mil. sec. 3)): Mark 1:4; John 1:25f,28; 3:22f,26; 4:2; 10:40; 1 Cor. 1:17; with the cognate noun τό βάπτισμα, Acts 19:4; ὁ βαπτίζων substantively equivalent to ὁ βαπτιστής, Mark 6:14 (24 T Tr WH). τινα, John 4:1; Acts 8:38; 1 Cor. 1:14,16. Passive *to be baptized*: Matt. 3:13f,16; Mark 16:16; Luke 3:21; Acts 2:41; 8:12,13,(36); 10:47; 16:15; 1 Cor. 1:15 L T Tr WH; 10:2 L T Tr marginal reading. WH marginal reading. Passive in a reflexive sense (i. e. middle, cf. Winer's Grammar, sec. 38, 3), *to allow oneself to be initiated by baptism, to receive baptism*: Luke (3:7,12); 7:30; Acts 2:38; 9:18; 16:33; 18:8 ; with the cognate noun τό βάπτισμα added, Luke 7:29; 1 aorist middle, 1 Cor. 10:2 (L T Tr marginal reading WH marginal reading ἐβαπτίσθησαν (cf. Winer's Grammar, sec. 38, 4 b.)); Acts

22:16. followed by a dative of the thing with which baptism is performed, ὕδατι, see bb. below. b. with prepositions; aa. εἰς, to mark the element into which the immersion is made: εἰς τόν Ἰορδάνην, Mark 1:9. to mark the end: εἰς μετάνοιαν, to bind one to repentance, Matt. 3:11; εἰς τό Ἰωάννου βάπτισμα, to bind to the duties imposed by John's baptism, Acts 19:3 (cf. Winer's Grammar, 397 (371)); εἰς ὄνομα τίνος, to profess the name (see ὄνομα, 2) of one whose follower we become, Matt. 28:19; Acts 8:16; 19:5; 1 Cor. 1:13, 15; εἰς ἄφεσιν ἁμαρτιῶν, to obtain the forgiveness of sins, Acts 2:38; εἰς τόν Μωυσῆν, to follow Moses as a leader, 1 Cor. 10:2. to indicate the effect: εἰς ἕν σῶμα, to unite together into one body by baptism, 1 Cor. 12:13; εἰς Χριστόν, εἰς τόν θάνατον αὐτοῦ, to bring by baptism into fellowship with Christ, into fellowship in his death, by which fellowship we have died to sin, Gal. 3:27; Rom. 6:3 (cf. Meyer on the latter passive, Ellicott on the former). bb. ἐν, with the dative of the thing in which one is immersed: ἐν τῷ Ἰορδάνῃ, Mark 1:5; ἐν τῷ ὕδατι, John 1:31 (L T Tr WH ἐν ὕδατι, but compare Meyer at the passage (who makes the article deictic)). of the thing used in baptizing: ἐν ὕδατι, Matt. 3:11; Mark 1:8 (T WH Tr marginal reading omit; Tr text brackets ἐν); John 1:26, 33; cf. Buttmann, sec. 133, 19; (cf. Winer's Grammar, 412 (384); see ἐν, I. 5 d. α.); with the simple dative, ὕδατι, Luke 3:16; Acts 1:5; 11:16. ἐν πνεύματι ἁγίῳ, to imbue richly with the Holy Spirit (just as its large bestowment is called an *outpouring*): Matt. 3:11; Mark 1:8 (L Tr brackets ἐν); Luke 3:16; John 1:33; Acts 1:5; 11:16; with the addition καί πυρί to overwhelm with fire (those who do not repent), i. e. to subject them to the terrible penalties of hell, Matt. 3:11. ἐν ὀνόματι τοῦ κυρίου, by the authority of the Lord, Acts 10:48. cc. Passive ἐπί (L Tr WH ἐν) τῷ ὀνόματι Ἰησοῦ Χριστοῦ, relying on the name of Jesus Christ, i. e. reposing one's hope on him, Acts 2:38. dd. ὑπέρ τῶν

182

νεκρῶν on behalf of the dead, i. e. to promote their eternal salvation by undergoing baptism in their stead, 1 Cor. 15:29; cf. (Winer's Grammar, 175 (165); 279 (262); 382 (358); Meyer (or Beet) at the passage); especially Neander at the passage; Rückert, Progr. on the passage, Jen. 18 47; Paret in Ewald's Jahrb. d. Biblical Wissensch. ix., p. 247; (cf. B. D. under the word Baptism XII. Alex.'s Kitto ibid. VI.).*

LEH Lexicon (A GREEK-ENGLISH LEXICON OF THE SEPTUAGINT, Revised edition 2003 Deutsche Bibelgesellschaft, Stuttgart)

1597 βαπτίζω
βαπτίζω+ - V 0-1-1-0-2-4
2 Kgs 5,14; Is 21,4; Jdt 12,7; Sir 34,25
M: *to dip oneself* 2 Kgs 5,14; *to wash* Jdt 12,7
ἡ ἀνομία με βαπτίζει *I am imbued with transgression* Is 21,4
Cf. DELLING 1970, 243-245; →NIDNTT; TWN

GIN Lexicon (Shorter Lexicon of the Greek New Testament F.Wilbur Gingrich second edition)

1137 βαπτίζω
βαπτίζω *dip, immerse*—**1.** of Jewish ritual washings, mid. and pass, *wash one's hands* Mk 7:4; Lk 11:38.—**2.** *baptize,* of ritual immersion by John the Baptist and Christians Mt 3:11, 13f, 16; 28:19; Mk 6:14, 24; J 4:1f; Ac 2:38 , 41; 8:12f, 36, 38; 1 Cor 1:14–17; 15:29.—**3.** fig. Mt 3:11; 1 Cor 10:2; 12:13. Of martyrdom Mk 10:38f. [pg 33]

Vines Expository Dictionary

Baptism, Baptist, Baptize [Verb]

baptizo "to baptize," primarily a frequentative form of bapto, "to dip," was used among the Greeks to signify the dyeing of a garment, or the drawing of water by dipping a vessel into another, etc. Plutarchus uses it of the drawing of wine by dipping the cup into the bowl (Alexis, 67) and Plato, metaphorically, of being overwhelmed with questions (Euthydemus, 277 D).

It is used in the NT in Luke 11:38 of washing oneself (as in 2 Kings 5:14, "dipped himself," Sept.); see also Isaiah 21:4, lit., "lawlessness overwhelms me." In the early chapters of the four Gospels and in Acts 1:5; Acts 11:16; Acts 19:4, it is used of the rite performed by John the Baptist who called upon the people to repent that they might receive remission of sins. Those who obeyed came "confessing their sins," thus acknowledging their unfitness to be in the Messiah's coming kingdom. Distinct form this is the "baptism" enjoined by Christ, Matt 28:19, a "baptism" to be undergone by believers, thus witnessing to their identification with Him in death, burial and resurrection, e.g., Acts 19:5; Rom 6:3,4; 1 Cor 1:13-17; 1 Cor 12:13; Gal 3:27; Col 2:12. The phrase in Matt 28:19, "baptizing them into the Name" (RV; cp. Acts 8:16, RV), would indicate that the "baptized" person was closely bound to, or became the property of, the one into whose name he was "baptized."

In Acts 22:16 it is used in the Middle Voice, in the command given to Saul of Tarsus, "arise and be baptized," the significance of the Middle Voice form being "get thyself baptized." The experience of those who were in the ark at the time of the Flood was a figure or type of the facts of spiritual death, burial, and resurrection, Christian "baptism" being an antitype, "a corresponding type," a "like

184

figure," 1 Pet 3:21. Likewise the nation of Israel was figuratively baptized when made to pass through the Red Sea under the cloud, 1 Cor 10:2. The verb is used metaphorically also in two distinct senses: firstly, of "baptism" by the Holy Spirit, which took place on the Day of Pentecost; secondly, of the calamity which would come upon the nation of the Jews, a "baptism" of the fire of Divine judgment for rejection of the will and word of God, Matt 3:11; Luke 3:16.

Questions

1. What language was the N.T. written in?
2. Why is it important to do a word study on baptism?
3. Are Lexicons infallible?
4. How did we get the English word baptism from the original Greek?
5. What are the two basic meanings of baptism?

186

I find it helpful to look at external sources to see how well they match up with the Bible. In this chapter, I will provide many quotes from early *Christian* writers who talked about baptism. These writers are not inspired and should not be treated as such. By examining these early writers, we learn what was being taught shortly after the Bible was written. Sometimes we will find they are teaching exactly what the Bible taught, and other times we can see how they have added their own opinions. However, when it comes to baptism, these early writers agree that a person must be baptized in water, and it is essential for salvation.

(A.D. 130) Barnabas:

Let us inquire if the Lord was careful to make a revelation in advance concerning the water and the cross. Concerning the water it was written with regard to Israel how they will not receive the baptism which brings forgiveness of sins but will supply another for themselves.... Blessed are those who placed their hope in his cross and descended into the water.... We descend into the water full of sins and uncleanness, and we ascend bearing reverence in our heart and having hope in Jesus in our spirit (11:1, 8, 11).

(A.D. 130) The Shepherd of Hermas:

The tower which you see being built is myself, the church. . .
Hear, then, why the tower has been built on the waters. Your
life .was saved and will be saved through water. The tower
has been founded by the pronouncement of his almighty and
glorious Name, and it is supported by the invisible power of
the Master (Vision III.iii.3).

"I have heard, Sir, from some teachers that there is no other
repentance except that one when we descended into the water and received the forgiveness of our former sins." He said
to me, "You heard correctly, for it is so. He who has received
forgiveness of sins ought to sin no more but to live in purity"
(Mandate IV.iii.l).

Therefore these also who have fallen asleep received the seal
of the Son of God and "entered into the kingdom of God."
For, he said, before a man bears the name of the Son of God
he is dead, but whenever he receives the seal, he puts away
mortality and receives life. The seal then is the water. They
descend then into the water dead and they ascend alive. The
seal itself, then, was preached to them also, and they made
use of it in order that they might "enter into the kingdom of
God." . . . These apostles and teachers who preached the
name of the Son of God, when they fell asleep in the power
and faith of the Son of God, preached also to those who had
fallen asleep before them and gave to them the seal of the
preaching. They descended therefore with them into the water and ascended again. The former went down alive and
came up alive, but the latter who had fallen asleep previously
went down dead but came up alive (Similitudes IX.xvi.3-6).

(A.D. 50–160) Didache: (Author of the writing is unknown.)

Concerning baptism, baptize in this way. After you have spoken all these things, "baptize in the name of the Father, and

of the Son, and of the Holy Spirit," in running water. If you do not have running water, baptize in other water. If you are not able in cold, then in warm. If you do not have either, pour out water three times on the head "in the name of the Father, and of the Son, and of the Holy Spirit." Before the baptism the one baptizing and the one being baptized are to fast, and any others who are able. Command the one being baptized to fast beforehand a day or two (Didache 7).

[Editor's note] Even though this is an early writing, we can see how the writer has added many things compared to what the Bible says about baptism. For instance, the Bible says nothing about using cold running water or having to fast before a person is baptized. The writer also offers pouring as an alternative when immersion is not possible. However, the Bible does not give an example or even hint as such an alternative. Despite the many additions this writer has made, it confirms these early *Christians* believed the baptism Jesus commanded (Mt. 28:19) was to be done in water.

(A.D. 150 - 160) Justin Martyr:

We shall explain in what way we dedicated ourselves to God and were made new through Christ lest by omitting this we seem to act improperly in our explanation. As many as are persuaded and believe that the things taught and said by us are true and promise to be able to live accordingly are taught to fast, pray, and ask God for the forgiveness of past sins, while we pray and fast with them. Then they are led by us to where there is water, and in the manner of the regeneration by which we ourselves were regenerated they are regenerated. For at that time they obtain for themselves the washing in water in the name of God the Master of all and Father, and of our Savior Jesus Christ, and of the Holy Spirit. For Christ also said: "Unless you are generated, you cannot enter the kingdom of heaven.... Since we have been born without our knowledge or choice at our first birth from the moist seed at the union of our parents and have existed in bad habits and evil conduct, in order that we might not remain children of ignorance and necessity but become children of choice and knowledge and might obtain in the water the forgiveness of past sins, there is called upon the one who chooses to be regenerated and who repents of his sins the name of God The Master of all and Father.... This washing is called illumination since they who learn these things are illuminated in their understanding (Apology I, 61).

For Christ, being "the firstborn of all creation," became also the beginning again of another race, who were born again by him through water, faith, and wood (that is, the mystery of the cross) (Dialogue 138:2).

By reason, therefore, of this laver of repentance and knowledge of God, which has been ordained on account of the transgression of God's people, as Isaiah cries, we have believed, and testify that that very baptism which he announced is alone able to purify those who have repented; and this is the water of life. ... For what is the use of that baptism which cleanses the flesh and body alone? Baptize the soul from wrath and from covetousness, from envy, and from hatred; and, lo! the body is pure (The Apostolic Fathers Dialogue with Trypho XIV).

And we, who have approached God through Him, have received not carnal, but spiritual circumcision, which Enoch and those like him observed. And we have received it through baptism, since we were sinners, by God's mercy; and all men may equally obtain it (The Apostolic Fathers Dialogue with Trypho XLIII).

But there is no other [way] than this; to become acquainted with this Christ; to be washed in the fountain spoken of by Isaiah for the remission of sin; and for the rest, to live sinless lives (The Apostolic Fathers Dialogue with Trypho XLIV).

Even as our Christ, by being crucified on the tree, and by purifying [us] with water, has redeemed us (The Apostolic Fathers Dialogue with Trypho LXXXVI).

Fragment of an Uncanonical Gospel:

You have washed in these running waters wherein dogs and swine have been cast night and day, and you have cleansed and wiped the outside skin which also the harlots and flute girls anoint, wash, wipe, and beautify for the lust of men, but within they are full of scorpions and all wickedness. But I and my disciples, who you say have not bathed, have been dipped in the waters of eternal life.... (Oxyrhynchus Papyri V:840).

(A.D. 180) Theophilus:

On the fifth day came into existence the living creatures in the waters, through which the manifold wisdom of God is made plain. For who would be able to count their multitude and variety? Moreover, the things which come from the waters were blessed by God, in order that this might be a sign that men were going to receive repentance and forgiveness of sins through water and the "washing of regeneration," namely all those who come to the truth and are born again, and receive blessing from God (To Autolycus II.xvi).

(A.D. 180) Irenaeus:

Now, this is what faith does for us, as the elders, the disciples of the apostles, have handed down to us. First of all, it admonishes us to remember that we have received baptism for remission of sins -in the name of God the Father, and in the name of Jesus Christ, the Son of God, who became incarnate and died and was raised, and in the Holy Spirit of God; and that this baptism is the seal of eternal life and is rebirth unto God, that we be no more children of mortal men, but of the eternal and everlasting God (Proof of the Apostolic Preaching).

And when we come to refute them, we shall show in its fitting-place, that this class of men have been instigated by Satan to a denial of that baptism which is regeneration to God, and thus to a renunciation of the whole [Christian] faith.... For the baptism instituted by the visible Jesus was for the remission of sins (The Apostolic Fathers Against Heresies Book I XXI).

But there are some of them who assert that it is superfluous to bring persons to the water, but mixing oil and water together, they place this mixture on the heads of those who are to be initiated. ... And this they maintain to be the redemption. ... Others, however, reject all these practices, and maintain that the mystery of the unspeakable and invisible power ought not to be performed by visible and corruptible creatures.... These hold that the knowledge of the unspeakable Greatness is itself perfect redemption (The Apostolic Fathers Against Heresies Book I XXI).

And then, again, when [do we bear] the image of the heavenly? Doubtless when he says, "Ye have been washed," believing in the name of the Lord, and receiving His Spirit (The Apostolic Fathers Against Heresies Book V XII).

"And [4854] dipped himself," says [the Scripture], "seven times in Jordan." [4855] It was not for nothing that Naaman of old, when suffering from leprosy, was purified upon his being baptized, but [it served] as an indication to us. For as we are lepers in sin, we are made clean, by means of the sacred water and the invocation of the Lord, from our old transgressions; being spiritually regenerated as new-born babes, even as the Lord has declared: "Except a man be born again through water and the Spirit, he shall not enter into the kingdom of heaven" (The Apostolic Fathers Fragments from the Lost Writings of Irenaeus XXXIV).

(A.D. 190) Clement of Alexandria:

Is Christ perfected by the washing and is he sanctified by the descent of the Spirit? It is so. The same thing also takes place in the case of us, for whom the Lord became the pattern. Being baptized we are illuminated, being illuminated we are made sons, being made sons we are perfected, being perfected we are made immortal.... This work is variously called a grace gift, illumination, perfection, washing. It is the washing through which we are cleansed of our sins, the grace gift by which the penalties for our sins are removed, the illumination through which the holy light of salvation is beheld, that is through which the divine is clearly seen.... Instruction leads to faith, and faith together with baptism is trained by the Holy Spirit.... We who have repented of our sins, renounced our faults, and are purified by baptism run back to the eternal light, children to their father (Instructor I.vi.25.3-26.2; 30.2; 32.1).

And such as is the union of the Word with baptism, is the agreement of milk with water; for it receives it alone of all liquids, and admits of mixture with water, for the purpose of cleansing, as baptism for the remission of sins (Fathers of Second Century The Instructor Book I Chapter VI).

Then within the same period John prophesied till the baptism of Salvation (Fathers of Second Century The Stromata, or Miscellanies Book I Chapter XX).

(A.D. 200) Tertullian:

Happy is our sacrament of water, in that, by washing away the sins of our early blindness, we are set free and admitted into eternal life!.... But we, little fishes, after the example of our

IChThUS Jesus Christ, are born in water (Ante-Nicene Fathers Volume III On Baptism Chapter I).

It has assuredly been ordained that no one can attain knowledge of salvation without baptism. This comes especially from the pronouncement of the Lord, who says, "Except one be born of water he does not have life (Ante-Nicene Fathers Volume Volume III).

Therefore, after the waters have been in a manner endued with medicinal virtue through the intervention of the angel, the spirit is corporeally washed in the waters, and the flesh is in the same spiritually cleansed (Ante-Nicene Fathers Volume III On Baptism Chapter V).

Baptism itself is a bodily act, because we are immersed in water, but it has a spiritual effect, because we are set free from sins (Ante-Nicene Fathers Volume III On Baptism).

There is no difference whether one is washed in the sea or in a pool, in a river or a fountain, in a reservoir or a tub, nor is there any distinction between those whom John dipped in the Jordan and those whom Peter dipped in the Tiber, unless that eunuch whom Philip dipped in the chance water found on their journey obtained more or less of salvation (Ante-Nicene Fathers Volume III On Baptism).

Unless a man have been reborn of water and Spirit, he shall not enter into the kingdom of the heavens," has tied faith to the necessity of baptism. Accordingly, all thereafter who became believers used to be baptized. Then it was, too, that Paul, when he believed, was baptized (Ante-Nicene Fathers Volume III).

We enter, then, the font once: once are sins washed away, because they ought never to be repeated (Ante-Nicene Fathers Volume III).

For the flesh is the clothing of the soul. The uncleanness, indeed, is washed away by Baptism (Ante-Nicene Fathers Volume III).

(A.D. 225) Origen:

In commenting on the crossing of the Red Sea he speaks of Christian baptism: The evil spirits seek to overtake you, but you descend into the water and you escape safely; having washed away the filth of sin, you come up a "new man," ready to sing the "new song" (Homilies on Exodus V:5).

Matthew alone adds the words "to repentance," teaching that the benefit of baptism is connected with the intention of the baptized person; to him who repents it is salutary, but to him who comes to it without repentance it will turn to greater condemnation (Ante-Nicene Fathers Volume 9).

(A.D. 250) Pseudo-Cyprian:

It follows therefore that Israel is condemned by the hand thrust toward the baptismal bath, and there it is witnessed what he believed. And after the reception of the seal purified by the Spirit, he prays to receive life through the food of thanksgiving, namely of the bread which comes from benediction.... Those learn who one time taught, they keep commandments who once commanded, are dipped who used to "baptize," and are circumcised who used to circumcise. Thus the Lord wanted the Gentiles to flourish. You see to what extent Christ has loved you (Against the Jews 10:79-82).

For he who has been sanctified, his sins being put away in baptism, and has been spiritually reformed into a new man, has become fitted for receiving the Holy Spirit; since the apostle says, "As many of you as have been baptized into Christ have put on Christ (Ante-Nicene Fathers Volume 5 Epistle LXXIII).

For the blessed apostle sets forth and proves that baptism is that wherein the old man dies and the new man is born, saying, "He saved us by the washing of regeneration (Ante-Nicene Fathers Volume 5 Epistle LXXIII).

But further, one is not born by the imposition of hands when he receives the Holy Ghost, but in baptism, that so, being already born, he may receive the Holy Spirit (Ante-Nicene Fathers Volume 5 Epistle LXXIII).

In the laver of saving water the fire of Gehenna is extinguished (Ante-Nicene Fathers Volume 5 Treatise VIII On Works and Alms).

In the baptism of water is received the remission of sins (Ante-Nicene Fathers Volume 5 Treatise XI Exhortation to Martyrdom, Addressed to Fortunatus).

That all sins are put away in baptism. In the first Epistle of Paul to the Corinthians: "Neither fornicators, nor those who serve idols, nor adulterers, nor effeminate, nor the lusters after mankind, nor thieves, nor cheaters, nor drunkards, nor revilers, nor robbers, shall obtain the kingdom of God. And these things indeed ye were: but ye are washed, but ye are sanctified in the name of our Lord Jesus Christ, and in the Spirit of our God (Ante-Nicene Fathers Volume 5 Testimonies).

Questions

1. Are the writings of these early writers inspired by God?
2. What can these early writers teach us about baptism?

American Heritage Dictionary of the English Language
http://www.bartleby.com/61/.

Ante-Nicene Fathers Vol. 1 (public domain)
http://biblefacts.org/ecf/indexv1.html.

Ante-Nicene Fathers Vol. 2 (public domain)
http://biblefacts.org/ecf/indexv1.html.

Ante-Nicene Fathers Vol. 3 (public domain
http://biblefacts.org/ecf/indexv1.html).

Ante-Nicene Fathers Vol. 5 (public domain)
http://biblefacts.org/ecf/indexv1.html.

Ante-Nicene Fathers Vol. 9 (public domain)
http://biblefacts.org/ecf/indexv1.html.

BDAG A GREEK-ENGLISH LEXICON OF THE NEW TESTAMENT AND OTHER EARLY CHRISTIAN LITERATURE. Third Edition Copyright © 2000 by The University of Chicago Press (electronic version).

Boles, H. Leo. *Acts of the Apostles* Nashville TN.: Gospel Advocate Company, 1964.

Burgon, John William. *The Last Twelve Verses of Mark's Gospel Vindicated* (public domain)
http://www.ccel.org/ccel/burgon/mark.txt.

Burton, H. David. *Baptism for the Dead*
www.lightplanet.com/mormons/temples/baptism.html.

BWHEBB, BWHEBL, BWTRANSH [Hebrew]; BWGRKL, BWGRKN, and BWGRKI [Greek] Postscript® Type 1 and TrueTypeT fonts Copyright © 1994-2006 BibleWorks, LLC. All rights reserved. These Biblical Greek and Hebrew fonts are used with permission and are from BibleWorks, software for Biblical exegesis and research. Any use of Bible Work's fonts must display the above information.

Clarke, B.J. *DOES MARK 16:9-20 BELONG IN THE BIBLE?* Studies in Mark . Ed. Dub McClish. Denton, Tx: Valid Publications, Inc., 2002. 615-660.

Coffman, James Burton. *Coffman Commentaries* ACU Press electronic edition.

Easton's Bible Dictionary Revised International Bible Translators, Inc. (electronic edition 1988).

Friberg ANALYTICAL LEXICON OF THE GREEK NEW TESTAMENT Baker Books 2000.

ISBE Electronic Edition Copyright © 1997 (electronic version).

Jackson, Wayne. christiancourier.com.

Jackson, Wayne. *The Acts of the Apostles* Stockton, CA.: Christian Courier Publications, 2005.

Jackson, Wayne. *Treasures from the Greek New Testament for the English Reader* Stockton, CA.: Courier Publications, 1996.

Kittel's Theological Dictionary Abridged Ed. Gerhand Kittle, Gerhand Friedrich, Geoffrey W. Bromiley. Wm. B. Eerdmans Publishing Co. 1985.

Louw-Nida Lexicon GREEK-ENGLISH LEXICON of the NEW TESTAMENT BASED ON SEMANTIC DOMAINS © 1988, 1989 by the United Bible Societies Second edition (electronic version).

Machen, J. Gresham. *New Testament Greek for Beginners* [Toronto, Canada: The Macmillan Company, 1923.]

Macknight, James. *Macknight on the Epistles* (Grand Rapids, MI.: Baker Book House, 1984).

Mare, W. Harold. *Mastering New Testament Greek* Grand Rapids: Baker, 1979.

McGarvey, J. W. *Original Commentary on Acts* http://studylight.org/com/oca/.

Nelson's New Illustrated Bible Dictionary Ed. Ronald F. Youngblood Thomas Nelson Publishers Copyright © 1995, 1986.

New Revised Standard Version Bible Copyright © 1989, Division of Christian Education of the National Council of the Churches of Christ in the United States of America.

NIV®. Copyright © 1973, 1978, 1984 by International Bible Society.

Padfield, David. *For The Remission of Sins* www.padfield.com.

Reese, Gareeth L. *New Testament History Acts* College Press Publishing Company, 2002. Robertson, A.T. *A GRAMMAR*

OF THE GREEK NEW TESTAMENT IN THE LIGHT OF HISTORICAL RESEARCH Ed. Tinsley Such, 3rd ed. Hodder & Stoughton (electronic version).

Schaff, Philip. *A Companion to the Greek New Testament and English Version* New York: Harper & brothers, 1883.

Schmiedel, Winer. *Grammatik* 8th ed. Leipzeig, Germany.

Summers, Ray. *Essentials of New Testament Greek* Nashville, Tennessee: Broadman, 1950

Thayer's Greek Lexicon (IBT) 1998-2000 (electronic version).

THE BOOK OF MORMON ANOTHER TESTAMENT OF JESUS CHRIST http://scriptures.lds.org/bm/contents.

The Doctrine and Covenants of the Church of Jesus Christ of Latter-day Saints http://scriptures.lds.org/bm/contents.

The Holy Bible, English Standard Version. Copyright © 2001,2007 by Crossway Bibles.

The New King James Version Copyright © 1982, Thomas Nelson, Inc. Used by permission. All right reserved. (All Scriptures are taken from the New King James version unless otherwise stated).

The Pulpit Commentary Hendrickson Publishing ,1985.

The Works of Flavius Josephus Translated by William Whiston http://www.ccel.org/j/josephus/works/JOSEPHUS.HTM.

UBS Lexicon GREEK-ENGLISH DICTIONARY OF THE NEW TESTAMENT © 1993.

Vines Expository Dictionary Of Old and New Testament Words Nashville TN.: Thomas Nelson Inc. http://vines.mike-obrien.net/.

Wharton, Edward. *The Distinct Nature of the Church* SIBI, 1992.

Woods, Guy N. *Gospel Advocate* September 1988.

Woods, Guy N. *Questions and answers* Henderson TN.: Freed-Hardeman College Lectures electronic edition.